GIMSON'S KINGS & QUEENS

BEING AN ACCOUNT OF EVERY SOVEREIGN FROM WILLIAM I TO
CHARLES III, INCLUDING SEVERAL DETAILS ONE WOULD LIKE
TO KNOW BUT MAY HAVE FORGOTTEN, SUCH AS WHERE THE
BUTT OF MALMSEY COMES IN, FOLLOWED BY A SHORT ACCOUNT
OF WHY THE MONARCHY HAS SURVIVED FOR SO LONG.

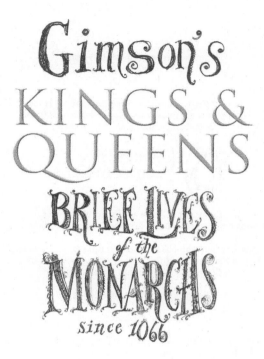

Gimson's
KINGS &
QUEENS
BRIEF LIVES
of the
MONARCHS
since 1066

illustrated by

Martin Rowson

◪ SQUARE PEG

Square Peg, an imprint of Vintage,
20 Vauxhall Bridge Road,
London SW1V 2SA

Square Peg is part of the Penguin Random House
group of companies whose addresses can be found
at global.penguinrandomhouse.com.

First published by Square Peg in 2015

www.vintage-books.co.uk

Quotation on p.243 from 'It was ludicrous but also magnificent'
by Rachel Cooke, published in the *Observer*, 6 May 2023

A CIP catalogue record for this book is available from the British Library

ISBN 9780224101196

Text designed by Lindsay Nash
Typeset in Quadraat by Palimpsest Book Production Ltd, Falkirk, Stirlingshire
Printed and bound in Great Britain by Clays Ltd, Elcograf S.p.A.

The authorised representative in the EEA is Penguin Random House Ireland,
Morrison Chambers, 32 Nassau Street, Dublin DO2 YH68

Penguin Random House is committed to a sustainable
future for our business, our readers and our planet. This book
is made from Forest Stewardship Council® certified paper.

MIX
Paper | Supporting
responsible forestry
FSC® C018179

For David Birt

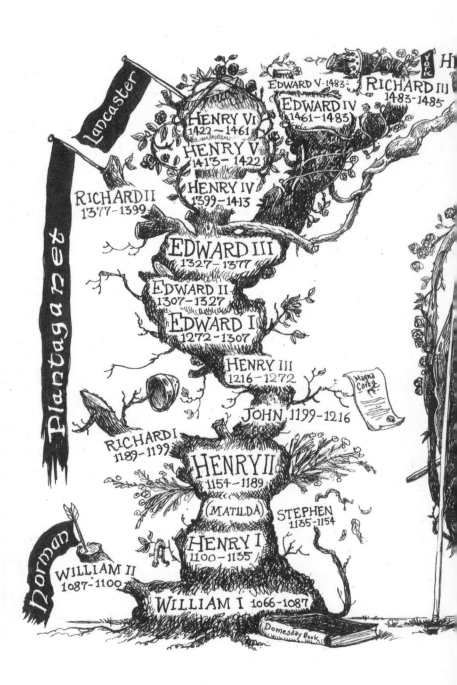

Lancaster

Plantagenet

Norman

EDWARD V·1483·
RICHARD III
1483-1485

HENRY VI
1422 – 1461
EDWARD IV
1461-1483

HENRY V
1413 – 1422

HENRY IV
1399 – 1413

RICHARD II
1377 - 1399

EDWARD III
1327 – 1377

EDWARD II
1307 – 1327

EDWARD I
1272 – 1307

HENRY III
1216 – 1272

Magna Carta

JOHN, 1199 – 1216

RICHARD I
1189 – 1199

HENRY II
1154 – 1189

(MATILDA)   STEPHEN
1135 – 1154

HENRY I
1100 – 1135

WILLIAM II
1087 - 1100

WILLIAM I 1066 - 1087

Domesday Book

The English will never love or honour their king, unless he be victorious and a lover of arms and war against their neighbours and especially against such as are greater and richer than themselves. Their land is more fulfilled of riches and all manner of goods when they are at war than in times of peace. They take delight and solace in battles and slaughter: covetous and envious are they above measure of other men's wealth.

JEAN FROISSART, 1400

A Subject and a Sovereign are clean different things.

CHARLES I, SPEECH BEFORE HIS EXECUTION, 1649

The influence of the Crown is not confined merely to political affairs. England is a domestic country. Here the home is revered and the hearth sacred. The nation is represented by a family – the royal family; and if that family is educated with a sense of responsibility and a sentiment of public duty, it is difficult to exaggerate the salutary influence they may exercise over a nation.

BENJAMIN DISRAELI, 1872

A few faults are indispensable to a really popular monarch.

GEORGE BERNARD SHAW

Our royal family is a rather absurd institution, no doubt. But then, humanity itself is rather absurd.

MAX BEERBOHM

As far as I can see, some people have to be fed royalty like sea-lions fish.

LADY STRATHMORE,
MATERNAL GRANDMOTHER OF ELIZABETH II

CONTENTS

INTRODUCTION

This slim volume contains brief lives of our last forty-one kings and queens, from 1066 to the present day. They met with triumph and disaster, but were very seldom boring, for they played a role which exercises an irresistible hold on the imagination. As J. H. Plumb remarks in *The First Four Georges*, 'It is almost impossible for a monarch to be dull, no matter how stupid.'

The book was prompted by the realisation that on 9 September 2015 Elizabeth II would become our longest-serving sovereign, surpassing Queen Victoria's record of sixty-three years and 216 days on the throne. Amid the celebrations of that landmark, many also wondered, without necessarily voicing the thought, how it is that the English and then British monarchy has survived for so long. For Elizabeth, and her heirs Charles, William and George, recall in their very names their forebears.

The story opens with an illegal immigrant, William the Conqueror, who never learned his new subjects' language, though he well understood how to compel their obedience and seize their lands. It continues with such extravagant figures as Richard the Lionheart, the greatest knight in Christendom, and Richard III, regarded by some as the greatest criminal. We see Henry VIII degenerate from a Renaissance prince into a tyrant, casting off wives and servants with merciless finality but making England independent of Rome. His daughter, Elizabeth I, upholds that independence by the heroic expedient of steering a middle course where none seemed to exist.

Charles I would not admit the need to find a middle course, so lost his head. William III, the Dutchman who became our most underestimated monarch, played a vital but forgotten role in the assertion of English liberty. Victoria turned the monarchy into the symbol of a new morality, and a new empire. Her great-great-granddaughter, Elizabeth II, survived the loss of that empire by practising Christian virtues which have become unfashionable.

Because the monarchy is seen as a source of stability, it is easy to fall into the error of imagining that its history must be stable. We glance at its family tree and find ourselves lost in admiration of the millennium of continuity which is there declared.

But look more closely, and one finds the story is marked by savage discontinuities: by family quarrels settled in battle or by murder and usurpation. These pages tell a tale of bastardy, courage, conquest, brutality, vanity, vulgarity, corruption, anarchy, absenteeism, piety, nobility, divorce, expropriation, execution, civil war, madness, magnificence, profligacy, frugality, philately, abdication, dutifulness, family breakdown and family revival.

The first aim of this volume is to entertain, not to instruct. It is not a textbook, and should not be used as an aid to passing exams, for its attitudes might annoy the examiners, and will distress professional historians who attach exaggerated importance to their own discoveries. Brevity has trumped comprehensiveness: the book cannot offer an adequate account of what was happening in Scotland, Wales and Ireland, or in many other fields of English life.

Between the ages of eight and thirteen, I was lucky to have a history master, David Birt, who taught his pupils the things it was a pleasure to know, and not just the things one ought to know. His favourite king was John (1199–1216), conventionally regarded as the worst in English history.

Thanks to his early teaching, I acquired some slight grasp of the whole sweep of English and British history, which I have ever since felt to be slipping from my not very retentive memory, so that gaps opened up where I had no idea what was going on. Although I read history at university, I found myself responding to any question about the past with the apologetic claim that it was 'not my period'. I no longer knew when the Plantagenets began, or indeed when they ended. The present volume might be described as a refresher course for those who used to know some history, and an introduction for those who never did.

There are many admirable biographies of individual monarchs. But I do not know of a recent, readable volume which covers them all in under 250 pages. The exception to this rule is 1066 and All That, which by redefining history as 'what you can remember' comes in at a more manageable 116 pages. But the running joke in that classic, namely that everything is misremembered, is not quite so funny now that most of us were never made to learn these things in the first place.

A Shortened History of England, by G. M. Trevelyan, published in 1942, is a masterpiece of Whig eloquence, the best of its kind ever written, but although an abridgement, it still stretches to 560 pages. The English and Their History, by Robert Tombs, published in 2014, offers a penetrating narrative informed by wide scholarship, but is 890 pages long. The great difficulty is to know what to leave out. But there is also a kind of liberation in deciding not to try to say everything.

I have called this volume Gimson's Kings & Queens – a vainglorious title – in order to emphasise that it offers a personal view. At the end of the book, I offer a few thoughts about why the British monarchy has lasted so long.

WILLIAM I
1066–1087

William I conquered England. This brave, clever, brutal, illiterate Norman warlord attained at the Battle of Hastings the most durable victory of any monarch in English history. At the head of 5,000 knights, he invaded and made himself master of a kingdom with perhaps 1.5 million inhabitants. The English ruling class was wiped out, its lands taken over by the invaders, and French replaced English as the language of government. William the Conqueror, as he became known, was able to pass on his throne to his sons and more remote descendants, who hold it to this day.

During the Hastings campaign, William had several strokes of luck. But for the most part, he made his own luck. To the rapacity of his Viking ancestors, who had seized Normandy from the kings of France, he added remarkable gifts of organisation, including organised brutality. 'This is what will happen to you if you don't back me,' he demonstrated with terrifying clarity to potential rebels as he imposed a mutilation or a famine.

William was born in about 1027, and known at first as William the Bastard, for his origins were not as grand as his later achievements might lead one to suppose. He was the illegitimate son of Duke Robert of Normandy, also called Robert the Devil, and of Arlette, whose father, Fulbert, was a tanner: a disgusting trade carried out by despised people, for it involved kneading the skins of animals for hours in water mixed with the dung of pigeons or of dogs. At Falaise, a town in Normandy about thirty miles from the sea, they will show you the trenches in the castle courtyard which were used to dye those skins, where Duke Robert is supposed to have seen Arlette treading them barefoot and bare-legged.

Duke Robert liked the look of Arlette, and she, one may suppose, liked the look of him. They were both about seventeen years old and soon she bore him a son, William. Robert did not marry Arlette, but a few years later she became the wife of a nobleman with whom she had several more children, including Odo of Bayeux, a pugnacious and avaricious man who would play a large part in the subjugation of England.

Bastardy was normal enough among the Norman upper classes, but the duke wished to ensure that his only son would inherit the duchy. So before setting out on a pilgrimage to Jerusalem, he made the counts of Normandy swear that if he died, they would be loyal to William. In the summer of 1035, while on his way home from Jerusalem, he fell ill and died at Nicaea in what is now Turkey.

At the age of eight, William the Bastard became Duke of

Normandy. His inheritance descended into anarchy, and for a dozen years he was in danger of assassination before he could achieve anything. But as a young man he restored the situation by moving against his enemies with speed, boldness and unflinching ferocity. In his early twenties, he besieged the town of Alençon. The holders of an outlying fort mocked him by hanging animal hides from the walls: a reference to his lowly origins as the bastard son of a tanner's daughter. William did not see the joke. He proceeded to capture the fort and thirty-two of its defenders, and, in full view of the townspeople, had their hands and feet cut off. Alençon surrendered.

In 1051, William married Matilda, the daughter of one of his most powerful neighbours, the Count of Flanders. She was tiny, scarcely more than four feet in height, while he was burly, five feet ten inches tall, a dauntless warrior with a harsh voice and reddish hair. Within a few years, he had made Normandy secure.

But his lust for power and possessions was not sated. Early in 1066, on learning that Harold had been chosen as king by the Anglo-Saxon Witan, or council, in succession to Edward the Confessor, he resolved to invade England and overthrow the newly crowned king.

William had a tenuous claim by blood to the English throne: his grandfather was the brother of Edward the Confessor's mother. But the duke set greater store by a promise he had extracted in 1064, when Harold was unlucky enough to be driven on to the shores of Normandy, becoming William's reluctant guest. Harold was only allowed to return home after swearing to help William obtain the throne of England on Edward's death.

Although this oath had been obtained under duress, the duke took Harold's breaking of it as a personal affront. All his nobles except William FitzOsbern nevertheless advised that the invasion of England would be far too risky.

William dismissed their warnings. He recruited a cosmopolitan band of adventurers, drawn from Brittany, Flanders and more distant parts of Europe as well as Normandy, and obtained the Pope's blessing for the gigantic act of plunder on which they were about to embark. The Church was the duke's ally in this venture. His own half-brother, Odo, whom he had made Bishop of Bayeux, led 120 knights in the campaign, and at Hastings swung a mace in order to comply with the Church's teaching that it was wrong for a priest to shed blood with a sword.

By summer the duke had built a fleet, but it was delayed by contrary winds. When it did sail, it was forced back by a storm, with loss of life. William had the corpses buried in secret and persisted. At last, on 27 September, the fleet sailed again.

During the night, William's ship, being the fastest, got separated from the rest of the fleet. There was consternation on board. William calmly ordered a large breakfast, which he ate on deck while the rest of his invasion force caught up.

When the Normans landed unopposed at Pevensey, between the present-day towns of Eastbourne and Hastings, William stumbled and fell flat on the beach. His followers were dismayed by this ill omen. But William rose to his feet, raised a handful of sand in the air and cried out that this was a sign of God's will that the Normans should grasp England.

The Anglo-Saxon *fyrd*, or militia, had been watching the coast for four months in fear of such an attack, but had gone home to get in the harvest. Harold himself had marched north to defend his kingdom against Harald Hardrada, King of Norway, who had invaded with a powerful army.

After winning the Battle of Stamford Bridge near York, Harold hurried south to confront the Normans. They had moved along the coast a few miles east from Pevensey, to Hastings, where William had constructed a castle. He took the precaution of staying close to his line of communication with Normandy, but ordered his followers to ravage the country inland: a way of provoking the English to do battle with him before his own supplies ran low.

On the morning of 14 October 1066, William sighted the English army, about equal in size to his own. Harold had a reputation for boldness and William was surprised to see that the English had taken up a strong defensive position, on top of a steep hill about seven miles north-west of Hastings, with marshy streams guarding both flanks.

William's counts were appalled. To advance was suicide; to retreat, an ignominious disaster. William immediately ordered an attack.

After several bloody repulses, the Norman army began a panicky retreat, which drew the English from their impregnable position. William pulled off his helmet by the nosepiece, so his men could see he was still alive. By this risky expedient, he rallied his forces and turned the tide of battle. Harold was killed, probably by an arrow through the eye. The Normans were rich in archers and in cavalry, which the English lacked. Harold's men had fought all day with valour, but now they were leaderless and fled into the forest.

William with characteristic boldness followed up this victory by advancing via Wallingford to London, where he received the submission of the principal citizens and had himself crowned on Christmas Day at Westminster Abbey. When the Normans and English inside the church acclaimed the new king, the soldiers who were standing guard outside, and were no doubt feeling jumpy in the presence of large crowds of unknown Londoners, thought the noise meant a revolt had broken out, and set fire to buildings surrounding the abbey. A riot ensued and most of the congregation fled. Even William was seen to tremble, but he insisted the service be carried through to the end. William the Bastard had become William the Conqueror.

In the twenty-one years that he ruled England, this self-made man showed he knew how to hold what he had seized. The Normans were the greatest military architects of their time. They built castles, many of which survive to this day, at all the most strategic points in England, so a small number of mounted knights could dominate a wide area. They built churches too: William supported the Church on the understanding that it would sanctify his rule. The English clergy were replaced with foreigners. Lanfranc, an Italian Benedictine who had served with distinction as Abbot of Bec in Normandy, became Archbishop of Canterbury.

The Conqueror rewarded the 5,000 knights who had fought for him with English lands, in return for which they had to bring a certain number of men to fight again for him when required. He made these followers pay homage directly to him, rather than via overlords, as happened on the continent. The English ruling class was dispossessed.

In the first years of his reign, William faced frequent uprisings. These he suppressed with his customary savage brutality. In the winter of 1069–70, having crushed a revolt at York he carried out the Harrying of the North: a programme of ferocious terror and devastation which fell equally on everyone, whether they had rebelled or not, and left famine in its wake. The north took a century to recover.

William the Conqueror's marriage was by all accounts harmonious – contemporaries believe he remained faithful to Matilda – and it was undoubtedly fruitful. With Matilda he sired nine children, but he displayed little sense of family, and fought his eldest son, Robert Curthose ('Short-arse'), in single combat, as well as falling out with his half-brother, Odo of Bayeux, imprisoning him for treason.

By 1085, England had largely submitted to its conqueror's rule and was peaceful enough for William to institute his greatest feat of administration: the compilation of the Domesday Book, which recorded landholdings down to the last acre and the last pig. William betrayed no sense of the mystique of kingship. He was determined to have an efficient inventory of his conquests, and used the excellent Anglo-Saxon civil service to provide one. The bandit knew the value of the bureaucrat.

William remained to the end as touchy about insults to his person as he had shown himself at Alençon. With age he became immensely obese, and while recovering from an illness, heard that the King of France had said 'the fat man was long a-lying in': the suggestion being he was pregnant and was about to go into labour. William retorted with grim menace that he would do his 'churching' – the ceremony after giving birth – in Paris.

He accordingly set out on a punitive expedition. At Mantes, west of Paris, his horse stumbled on a hot cinder, and William, his gut spilling over his saddle, was thrown against the pommel. His ribs were smashed and organs ruptured, and in September 1087 he died in agony. The king's servants stripped his body and deserted him. When he was buried at Caen, his corpse burst as it was being forced into too small a stone sarcophagus, and such an unbearable stench filled the church that the service had to be hurried to its close.

Here was a macabre end for a monarch who took himself with unwavering seriousness. One cannot pretend he would have made a great comedian, but he had all the qualities needed to become a severe and celebrated king.

WILLIAM II

1087–1100

William the Conqueror was survived by three sons: Robert Curthose, William Rufus and Henry. On his deathbed, he bequeathed Normandy to Robert, England to William, and £5,000 to Henry, along with the astute observation that the youngest son need only exercise patience to acquire the lands of both his brothers.

William Rufus was about thirty when he became king. According to William of Malmesbury, he had a red face, yellow hair, different-coloured eyes, and a stutter, especially when angry. He never married, fathered no children, and preferred attractive young male courtiers with fashionably pointed shoes who wore their hair long in the English style. About 900 years before gay rights were written into law, chroniclers had no hesitation in condemning him for immorality.

The new king was as brutal and belligerent as his father, but lacked his level-headed strength of purpose, and could never be trusted to keep a treaty. Either by force of arms or the payment of huge sums of money, he wanted to get his hands on his brother's lands in Normandy.

Before long, William Rufus became known as an intolerably greedy king, who milked the English for money, and allowed his followers to do the same. He favoured his uncle, Odo of Bayeux, but was double-crossed by him. After the English had helped William Rufus to take Odo's castle of Rochester, they clamoured for Odo's death: but William had given his knightly word to spare him and the Norman garrison, and did so.

In 1089, Lanfranc, the Archbishop of Canterbury, died, and with him the last restraining influence on William, who proceeded to ravage the possessions of the Church, which he treated as if they were his own. But shortly afterwards, he fell ill, and in the face of death, promised to mend his ways. He accepted the saintly Anselm as Archbishop of Canterbury.

William then recovered, and became as intolerable as ever. A characteristic episode occurred in 1094, when he proposed to invade Normandy. The Normans were by now distrustful of him, and refused to join the expedition, so William instead enlisted the English. Yet when they arrived at Hastings with ten shillings each for provisions, William took their money and sent them home.

In 1097, his older brother, Robert Curthose, joined the First Crusade. To raise money, he leased Normandy to William for 10,000 marks. William found this sum by acts of extortion, carried out against landlords, who in turn robbed their peasants, and against the Church, whose shrines were pillaged.

William Rufus was by now on appallingly bad terms with just about everyone. In 1100 he was murdered (or just possibly killed by accident) while hunting in the New Forest and his body, dripping blood all the way, was carried to Winchester on a cart. There the clergy refused to carry out any services for him: an unprecedentedly severe sanction. It was said of him: 'He was loathsome to almost all his people, and abominable to God.'

HENRY I

1100–1135

On 2 August 1100, when William Rufus was killed, his older brother, Robert Curthose, was away on crusade, but his younger brother, Henry, was conveniently close at hand. He rode to Winchester, seized the royal treasury with drawn sword and persuaded some Witan members who were present to confirm him as king. Henry hastened to London and was crowned on 5 August: the fastest coronation in English history.

The new king entrenched his support by issuing a coronation charter in which he remedied the abuses of the last reign. A century later, this was to become one of the foundations of Magna Carta. Henry restored the coinage, which had been debased. He regularised measures: a yard is the distance from Henry's nose to his outstretched thumb. He filled bishoprics, which William Rufus had kept empty in order to seize the revenues, and restored Anselm, who had been in exile, as Archbishop of Canterbury.

Although Henry then quarrelled with Anselm about Church appointments, he remained on good personal terms with him. After Anselm's death he kept the see of Canterbury vacant for five years in order to pinch the revenues.

Henry was a calm-eyed administrator with an unusually good head for business. Nowadays he would be running a multinational corporation, and would leave the share price higher than when he took over. He had been born in 1068 in Yorkshire, the only English-born of the Norman kings. He was well educated, was known as Beauclerc, and spoke fluent English as well as understanding Latin. Though affable, he was described as 'the great dissembler', for it was hard to read his intentions. He was highly sexed and had many bastard children.

His harsh rule was beneficial to the country. He travelled with his court, dispensing justice in the mornings and devoting the afternoons to hunting. To counteract the influence of the barons, he brought in 'new men'. He sent out travelling judges on assize, and for finance he introduced the exchequer, named after the chequered cloth, laid across a large table, on which revenues were reckoned with counters.

In 1103, many barons deserted to Robert Curthose, who had returned from the Crusade. Henry did a deal with his older brother – always cheaper than war – and over the next seven years gradually suppressed the rebellious nobles. Like any good business-man, he was always prepared to wait for the opportune moment.

In 1106, Henry defeated Robert Curthose at the Battle of Tinchebrai in Normandy. He kept his brother imprisoned until Robert's death in 1134. Normandy now passed under the control of the English crown. In 1108, a Norman lord challenged Henry to single combat. Henry, ever the realist, refused.

Henry married Matilda, sister of King Edgar of Scotland. They had a son, William, and a daughter, Matilda. From 1117 to 1120, he campaigned in Normandy, where he achieved his aims by bribery and stratagem, and by the marriage of his only son William into the house of Anjou.

But in 1120, William set out from Normandy to England in the *White Ship*, a fast new vessel under an experienced captain, Thomas Fitzstephen. The passengers and crew were drunk even before at night this floating party of the Norman upper classes set sail. William gave orders that they should overtake the king, who had set sail earlier and was somewhere ahead.

Instead the *White Ship* hit a rock. Fitzstephen got William into a small boat and pushed off with some sailors. William heard his half-sister calling to him for help, and ordered the sailors to turn back. The boat was swamped by the multitude who tried to clamber aboard. All but two of the 300 people on the *White Ship* drowned.

This disaster sprang, like the sinking of the *Titanic*, from over-confidence, but was to have far more terrible ramifications. Henry fainted when he heard the news. He now had only a daughter, Matilda, to inherit the throne.

England had never yet been ruled by a queen. Henry was never-theless determined to ensure that she would succeed him. Twice he made all the barons vow to support her. But in 1130 he married

Matilda to Geoffrey of Anjou: a foreigner to the English and Norman barons, and not popular.

In 1135, Henry was taken ill while hunting, and a week later he died at Rouen. His doctor said his death was caused by eating a surfeit of lampreys. Modern medical opinion is that he died of a heart attack.

Stephen

1135–1154

Although Stephen of Boulogne, son of William the Conqueror's daughter Adela, had sworn to uphold Matilda's claim to the crown, as soon as Henry was dead he sailed to England and claimed it for himself. He was in some respects an admirable knight: brave, straightforward, charming and popular. He also possessed an instinct for self-preservation: he had taken one look at the crew of the *White Ship* and refused to sail in her.

But he was unfit to be king. He was too soft to cope with the double-dealings, treacheries and shifting alliances of the power-hungry nobility. Nor was he able to impose his authority on cousin Matilda. A prolonged power struggle broke out between Stephen and Matilda, and England descended into the horrors of civil war.

In the *Anglo-Saxon Chronicle*, a monk at Peterborough records the bitter experience of these nineteen years with a directness no paraphrase can match. He recounts how the barons behaved, once they saw that Stephen would let them get away with anything:

When the traitors understood that he was a mild man, and soft, and good, and no justice executed, then did they all wonder. They had done him homage, and sworn oaths, but they no truth maintained. They were all forsworn, and forgetful of their troth; for every rich man built his castles, which they held against him: and they filled the land full of castles. They cruelly oppressed the wretched men of the land with castle-works; and when the castles were made, they filled them with devils and evil men. Then took they those whom they supposed to have any goods, both by night and by day, labouring men and women, and threw them into prison for their gold and silver, and inflicted on them unutterable tortures; for never were any martyrs so tortured as they were. Some they hanged up by the feet, and smoked them with foul smoke; and some by the thumbs, or by the head, and hung coats of mail on their feet. They tied knotted strings about their heads, and twisted them till the pain went to the brains. They put them into dungeons, wherein were adders, and snakes, and toads; and so destroyed them. Some they placed in a crucet-house; that is, in a chest that was short and narrow, and not deep; wherein they put sharp stones, and so thrust the man therein, that they broke all the limbs.

The evils of a weak king exceeded those of a strong one. Stephen nevertheless hoped that he could arrange for his son, Eustace, to succeed him. But in 1153, Eustace died, and a negotiated peace became possible. Under the Treaty of Westminster, it was agreed that Stephen would rule for the rest of his life, but would be succeeded by Matilda's son, Henry. Soon afterwards, Stephen died, at the end of one of the most disastrous reigns in English history.

Henry II
1154–1189

In 1154 Henry of Anjou became King of England. He was twenty-one years old, and his lands stretched from Hadrian's Wall to the Pyrenees, thanks to the vast inheritances he had received from his parents and his wife.

Henry was already married to Eleanor of Aquitaine, a very rich, beautiful, energetic and unscrupulous woman eleven years older than himself. She had found her first husband, Louis VII, King of France, sexually unattractive, and was said to have slept, among a number of other men, with her uncle, Raymond of Antioch. Her baggage train when she accompanied Louis on the Second Crusade was so large that it impaired his army's mobility. In 1152 she persuaded the Pope to annul her marriage to Louis, and got married to Henry instead. Troubadours in Germany sang songs about how wonderful it would be 'to have England's Queen lie close in my arms'.

Henry II was a grandson of Henry I, whose daughter, Matilda, had married Geoffrey of Anjou, known also as Geoffrey Plantagenet, because of the sprig of broom, or *planta genista*, he wore in his cap. So Henry II was the first of England's Plantagenet kings.

On ascending the throne, Henry set about restoring peace to England. He was a short but strongly built man of immense energy, determination and ability, who spent his life constantly on the move with his court: one observer described him as a human chariot who drew everyone else along, another said he exhausted the whole court by keeping them standing all the time. He had a passion for hunting, and was known as 'a great connoisseur of hounds and hawks'.

The new king showed from the first that he was determined to be obeyed, and to enforce the efficient collection of royal revenues. He had the illegal castles of unruly barons torn down: no longer were they able to terrorise their localities. He liked to administer justice in person, but twenty-one of his thirty-five years as King of England were spent in his continental territories, so he also built a system which could function in his absence and which incorporated elements of Anglo-Saxon practice. During his reign, the English common law began to emerge. Peace returned to the land: a chronicler, William of Newburgh, asserted that a virgin could walk from one end of the realm to the other with her bosom full of gold, and come to no harm.

Henry appointed Thomas à Becket, an ambitious and able cleric who was the son of a prosperous London merchant, as his chancellor, or chief minister. The two men became boon companions. William Fitzstephen, who knew Becket well, describes them riding together down a London street on a cold winter's day, against which they are opulently dressed.

They come upon a ragged beggar, and Henry says: 'Would it not be a good deed to provide yonder beggar with warm clothing?'

Becket: 'Indeed, My Lord.'

Henry: 'Then you shall do this good deed!' And with these words, Henry leans over and starts to pull off Becket's magnificent scarlet cloak lined with grey fur. Becket, who owes everything to Henry, resists, and a wrestling match develops, with the two figures swaying this way and that, so that it seems one or other of them must be unhorsed.

Becket at last gives way, and the king throws the cloak to the amazed beggar, who hastens away praising God. That night, Henry tells the story to his court, amid much laughter at Becket's expense. The king has reminded everyone, with his joke, that he is in charge.

But Henry was enraged that his royal writ only ran in two-thirds of his kingdom: the remaining third, which belonged to the Church, was a law unto itself. Criminous clerks – clerics who had committed grievous offences, including, it was said, over a hundred murders since Henry became king – were tried in Church courts, which often imposed the lightest of penalties.

The king devised an ingenious plan to curb the Church's power and render it subservient to himself. He would appoint Becket, his faithful friend, Archbishop of Canterbury. The Pope resisted this scheme, and so did Becket. But Henry overruled them and in June 1162 Becket was enthroned as archbishop.

Becket now became as staunch a defender of the Church's rights as he had previously been of Henry's. He had turned from pleasure-loving courtier into pious ecclesiastic. He was intolerable. For eight years, Henry strove to bring the archbishop under control. For six of those years, Becket was in exile at various abbeys in Burgundy. In 1170, there came a cautious peace, and Becket returned to Canterbury, where he at once reverted to outspoken and intransigent defiance.

Henry spent Christmas in Normandy. Here three bishops arrived to complain about Becket, who had excommunicated them for taking part in the coronation of the Young King: a ceremony of French origin, in which Henry's eldest son was crowned as heir to the throne.

The king's rage against Becket bubbled over, and he is supposed to have cried: 'Who will rid me of this turbulent priest?'

Four knights slipped away from the royal household and made for Canterbury. When Henry realised they had gone, he sent messengers to bring them back.

On the evening of 29 December 1170, as the monks of Canterbury were preparing for vespers, the four knights entered the cathedral and demanded: 'Where is Thomas Becket, traitor to the king and realm?'

Becket replied: 'I am here, no traitor to the king but a priest. Why do you seek me? I am ready to suffer in His name, who redeemed me by His blood.'

The knights struck Becket's head with their swords, inflicting such wounds that 'the blood white with brain and the brain red with blood dyed the surface of the Virgin Mother Church'.

All Europe was shocked by the murder. Henry himself was appalled, and did penance. Dressed in sackcloth, the king walked barefoot through the streets of Canterbury. When he reached the archbishop's tomb, he had himself scourged by all the bishops and abbots who were present, and also by the eighty monks of Christ Church Priory. One suspects this beating was symbolic rather than fierce, or the king would have been half dead. Becket was venerated for the next 350 years as England's greatest saint and martyr, until his magnificent and highly profitable shrine at Canterbury Cathedral was destroyed on the orders of Henry VIII.

For over thirty years, Henry II was able to subdue every rival except the Church. He even conquered a large part of Ireland. But at length he was undone by his own sons, whom he had always spoiled.

These gangsters were not prepared to wait for their father to divide his possessions between them at his death. They fought against him, and against each other. Two of them, Henry and Geoffrey, died before he did, but that left Richard and John, both of whom were destined to become King of England.

Eleanor sided with her sons against their father. Henry imprisoned his estranged wife, and for a long time defeated his estranged sons. But in 1189, Richard again rebelled against Henry, who was heartbroken to discover that his youngest and most beloved son, John, had joined the rebels. The king went down in sorrow to the grave. His last recorded words were 'Shame, shame on a conquered king!'

He was buried at Fontevrault Abbey in Anjou, a foundation to which the Plantagenets made great benefactions. For it should be remembered that although Henry II had rescued England from anarchy, and begun to develop the system of trial by jury which would become an essential element in English justice, he had done so as a foreigner.

RICHARD I

1189–1199

Richard I was the most famous knight errant of his age, and perhaps of any age. He was called Coeur de Lion, or Lionheart, in recognition of his valour, and looked the part: over six feet tall, immensely strong, with blue eyes and reddish gold hair. He spent only ten months of his ten-year reign in England, where he complained about the weather, but he became one of the great English heroes.

Shortly before Richard ascended the throne, Jerusalem had fallen to the Seljuk Turks led by Saladin. Richard was the first prince to volunteer to help retake it: going on crusade offered an impeccably religious motive for glory, fighting and pillage. As the troubadour Pons de Capdeuil put it: 'What more can kings desire than the right to save themselves from hellfire by powerful deeds of arms?'

Richard was already an experienced soldier. Born in 1157, he was brought up at the court of his mother, Eleanor of Aquitaine, in Poitiers, which was famous for its songs of chivalry and courtly love. But these romantic notions did not inhibit Richard from behaving in an unchivalrous manner when it suited him.

At the age of sixteen he rebelled against his father, Henry II, after which he spent several years subduing Aquitaine, where he took castle after castle. This was his school of warfare, where he proved himself a brilliant and inspiring commander who was generous to his followers. Those who defied him had their hands cut off, their eyes gouged out, their women raped.

In September 1189, Richard was crowned in Westminster Abbey. He gave orders that no woman or Jew was to be present at the banquet which followed. Some of the principal Jews of London came to present gifts to him, but were set upon by the mob, which burned down their houses in Old Jewry and killed all those who attempted to escape the flames. Massacres followed in other parts of England, the worst in York, where 400 Jews killed themselves rather than convert to Christianity.

Henry II had left England prosperous after years of peace. Richard's only use for the place was to raise vast sums of money to finance the Third Crusade. He said he would sell London if he could find anyone rich enough to buy it.

According to G. M. Trevelyan, 'the solid part of the baronage' did not wish to accompany the king on this expedition to the Holy Land, and instead stayed at home to govern the island in his absence. Richard himself sailed from Dover in December 1189, having received the traditional pilgrim's staff and scrip, or leather satchel.

In June 1190, he joined the French king, Philip Augustus, at Vézelay, in Burgundy, and made a deal to split all proceeds of the Crusade half and half. In September, Richard sailed into Messina with his army and demanded the release of his sister, Joan, who was being held prisoner by Tancred, King of Sicily. Richard also demanded a large sum of money from Tancred, who baulked at this but was eventually forced to give in. Philip Augustus had likewise arrived at Messina, having marched overland from France, and the two foreign armies got into a row with the locals about women. Richard became annoyed, stormed Messina and raised his banner over it. His high-handed behaviour infuriated Philip Augustus, for the banner was a signal for loot.

Richard's rejection, after a long betrothal, of Philip Augustus' sister, Alys, made matters worse. On his way to the Holy Land, Richard got married in Cyprus to his new betrothed, Berengaria of Navarre. He wore a mantle of striped silk decorated with gold crescents and silver suns, with a scarlet hat embroidered with golden birds and beasts. His leggings were of cloth of gold and on his heels were gilded spurs.

Berengaria had been selected for him by his mother, Eleanor of Aquitaine, and he appears to have spent very little time with her. The joys of the marriage bed were for Richard as nothing compared to the joys of the battlefield, and they had no children. This has led to speculation that he was gay, especially as a hermit once warned him against the sin of Sodom. But medieval hermits could be almost as excitable about such matters as modern historians.

In three months, Richard conquered Cyprus, including its supposedly impregnable hill fortresses. The ruler of the island, a ropey character called Isaac Comnenus who was a cousin of the Emperor of Byzantium, surrendered on condition that he was not put in iron fetters. Richard agreed, and instead put him in silver chains.

By the time Richard arrived at the Muslim-held port of Acre, it had been under Christian siege for almost two years. He reinvigorated the attackers and in July 1191, Acre fell. Richard, Philip Augustus and Leopold of Austria, who was leading the remnants of a German force, all raised their banners over the captured city, but English soldiers threw Leopold's banner into a ditch. Leopold returned home in a huff, and Philip Augustus set off back to France.

Richard had captured 2,700 men, women and children in Acre. He threatened to behead these Muslims unless Saladin agreed to exchange them for the True Cross, supposedly a piece of the actual cross on which Jesus had been crucified, and for some Christian prisoners. Saladin played for time, so Richard had the massacre carried out. There was a military reason for doing so: Richard did not wish, in his advance on Jerusalem, to be encumbered by a large number of prisoners, or else leave them somewhere behind him.

But it is also true that in those days, Christians might slay the infidel with as little remorse as Islamic State now shows. David Hume, in his great *History of England*, which 250 years after it appeared can still be read with pleasure, draws the following contrast between the Crusaders and the Saracens, as their adversaries were known:

The advantage indeed of science, moderation, humanity, was at that time entirely on the side of the Saracens . . . this gallant emperor [Saladin], in particular, displayed, during the course of the war, a spirit and generosity, which even his bigoted enemies were obliged to acknowledge and admire. Richard, equally martial and brave, carried with him more of the barbarian character; and was guilty of acts of ferocity, which threw a stain on his celebrated victories.

Although Richard's atrocity at Acre is remembered with fury in the Muslim world, he also won his enemies' respect. Saladin's biographer, Baha' ad-Din, wrote of him: 'Richard was a man of great courage and spirit. He fought great battles and showed a burning passion for war. His wealth, reputation and valour were greater than the French king . . . God alone was able to save us from his malice; never have we had to face a bolder or subtler opponent.'

In October 1191, Richard advanced down the coast towards Jerusalem, harassed by the Saracens. On the way, he won the Battle of Arsuf: 'There the fierce, extraordinary king cut down the Turks in every direction, and none could escape the force of his arm, for wherever he turned, brandishing his sword, he carved a wide path for himself, cutting them down like a reaper with his sickle.'

By December 1191, he was within twelve miles of Jerusalem. But although heedless of his own safety, he would not risk his small army in an assault, and instead turned back towards the coast. In February 1192, he concluded a three-year truce with Saladin: for Richard knew that his younger brother, John, and Philip Augustus of France were attempting in his absence to seize his lands.

But how, given that he was now on such bad terms with both Leopold and Philip Augustus, was he to get back home? He set out by ship, was driven on to the Adriatic coast and proceeded overland in disguise with a few companions. But Richard was uncommonly tall, his bearing was regal, and with his usual disregard for personal danger, he wore jewelled gloves and a kingly ring. At Christmas 1192 in Austria, his disguise was penetrated and he was captured by Leopold.

According to a thirteenth-century legend, Blondel, a troubadour who was a friend of Richard, set out to discover where the king was.

He heard that the castle of Dürnstein held a special prisoner, so sang beneath the window a song which only he and Richard knew. When Blondel heard an answering voice, he knew he had found the king.

This story used to be known by every English schoolchild, and there is no doubt that Richard loved music, was on good terms with many troubadours and himself wrote poetry in French and Provençal. But later historians point out that negotiations for Richard's ransom began at once, so there was no need for a minstrel to establish his whereabouts.

The immense sum of 150,000 marks, or thirty-four tons of silver, was paid for his release, and in March 1194 he landed at Sandwich, in Kent. With characteristic swiftness he reasserted his authority in England, and by May that year was conducting military operations in Normandy, where John, with his usual fickleness, deserted Philip Augustus and prostrated himself before Richard, who proceeded to forgive his brother for being treacherous in his absence.

From 1194 to 1199, Richard campaigned with complete success in Normandy and Aquitaine, and recovered all the lands seized by Philip Augustus. But in March 1199, Richard besieged the footling fort of Châlus, which had a handful of ill-equipped defenders. Richard, without his armour, inspected the defences, and was hit in the shoulder by a bolt fired by the one crossbowman on the other side. While gangrene set in, the fort was taken, and the crossbowman was brought before Richard, who pardoned him. Soon afterwards the king died, at the age of forty-one, where-upon his enraged troops flayed the crossbowman alive.

Saladin said of Richard: 'I have long been aware that your king is a man of honour and very brave, but he is absurdly rash in the way that he plunges into the midst of danger, and in his reckless indifference to his own safety.' This superb indifference to danger led to Richard's death, but was also one of the qualities that won him universal esteem.

JOHN
1199–1216

King John provoked, by his many bad qualities, a greater weight of condemnation than any other English monarch before Richard III. The chronicler Matthew Paris expressed the prevailing view: 'Foul as it is, hell itself is defiled by the presence of King John.' He was so untrustworthy, devious, suspicious of his subjects, severe in his exactions and unsuccessful in his campaigns that he at length united a great part of the baronage against him, and was forced to agree to Magna Carta. The paradox of his reign was that by combining immorality with incompetence, he caused the drafting of a document which came to be seen as the foundation of English and American liberties.

John was the youngest of the five sons and three daughters of Henry II and Eleanor of Aquitaine. He was born in 1167 and nicknamed Lackland, for it seemed at first that he would inherit nothing. He rebelled both against his father and against Richard I, who by 1189 was his only surviving brother. Richard learned, while away on crusade, of John's treachery, and remarked in an unconcerned tone: 'My brother John is not the man to conquer a country if there is anyone to offer the feeblest resistance.'

When Richard got home, John begged for and received his forgiveness, and fought with him against the French king, Philip Augustus: the very man with whom John had previously been allied. In 1199, the dying Richard named John as his heir, even though their nephew Arthur, son of their dead brother Geoffrey, in theory had a better claim.

John proceeded to attempt to safeguard his enormous continental possessions by signing on soft terms a treaty with Philip Augustus. Because of this deal, the English barons conferred on John the contemptuous nickname of Softsword. Soon afterwards the thirty-three-year-old English king was so violently attracted by the thirteen-year-old Isabella of Angoulême that he became determined to marry her. This was for several reasons a bad idea. John had to have his marriage to his English wife, Isabella of Gloucester, annulled; he inflicted a grievous insult on Hugh de Lusignan, the powerful nobleman to whom Isabella of Angoulême had previously been betrothed; and he spent so much time in bed with his new wife that, according to the chroniclers, this contributed to the loss of Normandy.

In 1203, John won a brilliant victory at Mirebeau, near Tours, in which he captured his nephew, Arthur, and many other knights. But he proceeded to treat these prisoners so badly that, as so often in his career, he threw away the advantage he had gained. Worst of all was the king's treatment of Arthur, who was now sixteen, and being held at Falaise.

John, who believed some of his barons were conspiring with his nephew against him, reckoned the best way to render him unfit ever to become king was to have him blinded and castrated. When John's servants told Arthur what they were going to do, he burst into tears, and persuaded them to spare him. But Arthur was now taken to Rouen, and after that he vanished. It was said that John himself, 'whilst drunk and possessed of the Devil', murdered his nephew, tied a heavy stone to the corpse and flung it into the Seine. This affair left a deep stain on John's reputation, for whether or not he had carried out the murder himself, he was plainly responsible for Arthur's disappearance.

Nor was he able to retrieve the situation, as his brother Richard would have done, by a string of glorious victories. By 1204 John had lost most of the territories on the mainland of Europe which he had inherited only five years before. He retreated to England, where he imposed heavy taxes in order to raise enough money to reconquer the traditional Plantagenet lands on the continent. At every level of society, from the wealthiest cleric to the lowliest peasant, the pain of his exactions was felt.

From 1205 John picked a quarrel with Pope Innocent III about the appointment of the Archbishop of Canterbury. The Pope chose Stephen Langton, a man with exceptional gifts as a leader. John retaliated by appropriating the revenues of Canterbury and forcing the monks into exile. In 1208, Innocent placed England under an interdict: all church services were suspended except baptism and hearing the confession of those who were dying. John retaliated by seizing Church property. Innocent excommunicated the king, which amounted to an invitation to rebel against him. In 1212 the Welsh rose against John, the Irish and the Scots were restless and there were rumours of plots among the English barons. The Pope now called on the French king to depose John.

Philip Augustus prepared an army at Boulogne, but John confounded him by declaring that he would become the Pope's vassal and pay him 1,000 marks a year. This meant that an invasion would constitute an attack on the Pope's own property, so Philip Augustus had to call the whole thing off. John belatedly accepted Langton as Archbishop of Canterbury, and in June 1214 the interdict was lifted. But Langton and many others disapproved of John's gift of England to the Pope.

John attempted to regain by force of arms his family's lands in what is now France. But his allies were defeated in July 1214 at the Battle of Bouvines, and he returned to England to find himself in a weaker position than ever. Rebellious barons began quoting the coronation charter approved by Henry I in 1100. In April 1215, Archbishop Langton relayed the barons' demands to John, who rejected them with the words, 'Why not ask for my kingdom?' He ordered the confiscation of the rebels' estates, but they responded by marching on London and plundering it. On 27 May, John asked Langton to arrange a truce. This was done, and a meeting followed at Runnymede, on the Thames near Windsor, on 15 June 1215.

Here the Great Charter, or Magna Carta, was agreed. It was a peace treaty, and as such it had an inherent weakness: the barons had no way of enforcing the king's obedience to it except by making war on him. But it contained two principles to which later opponents of arbitrary royal power could appeal with great effect. One was the promise that the king 'will not prosecute any man except by lawful judgement of his peers': the right to trial by jury. The other was the assurance that no tax would be raised 'unless by common council of our kingdom', which afterwards developed into the principle of 'no taxation without representation'.

Magna Carta set out to limit the power of the king, by stating rights which were considered already to exist. This meant that in centuries to come, opponents of royal power could not be dismissed as revolutionaries who wanted to tear down legitimate authority: they could claim to be conservatives, who were upholding ancient rights which had existed even before the Norman Conquest.

But in the short term, John proved as impossible as ever to restrain. The Pope, who was now on his side, urged him to reject Magna Carta, while the barons looked to Louis Capet, the son of the French king, for help. In May 1216, Louis entered London unopposed. John managed to commit a final act of folly. While crossing the Wash with his army, he lost his entire baggage train and his crown. Shortly after this disaster, he died of apoplexy brought on by gorging himself on peaches and new cider. He was buried at Worcester. Osbert Lancaster observes in his account of John that 'his sole redeeming feature seems to have been like so many celebrated criminals, he was invariably kind to his mother'.

HENRY III

1216–1272

Henry III was only nine years old when his father, King John, unexpectedly died, leaving the country in chaos. Rebel barons held much of the east, the French under Louis Capet, heir to the King of France, occupied London and Winchester, and in the north the Scots were mounting an invasion.

Henry's mother, Isabella of Angoulême, was at Gloucester, and hastened to have him crowned. No crown was available, so the boy wore a piece of her jewellery: a golden chaplet or bracelet. Nor could an archbishop be found, so she got Peter des Roches, the Bishop of Winchester, to conduct the coronation, which took place in Gloucester Abbey, now the cathedral.

John's son has gone down in history as a weak king, useless as a soldier, a poor judge of political situations and dominated by the more powerful personalities around him. Yet he reigned for longer than any English monarch before George III, and rather surprisingly he died in his bed. For weakness is not in every circumstance a drawback. With John dead, the barons lacked an opponent so bad he could be used to justify almost any act of rebellion. They no longer thought it might be preferable to be ruled by the King of France.

And the men who ruled England during Henry's minority knew how to save him from being punished for the sins of his father. They issued a letter in which the boy king said: 'We hear that a quarrel arose between our father and certain nobles of our kingdom, whether with justification or not we do not know. We wish to remove it forever since it has nothing to do with us.' Magna Carta, repudiated by John, was reissued, though without the clauses allowing the barons to rebel if the king failed to observe it.

William the Marshal, Henry III's first regent, was an accomplished soldier who had served every king since Henry II. He routed the French and the rebel barons at the Battle of Lincoln, and forced the French to leave England. He was succeeded by Hubert de Burgh, who had commanded the English ships that at the Battle of Dover defeated a French fleet which was bringing reinforcements. In 1220, Henry was given a second coronation, at Westminster Abbey, where Stephen Langton, one of the great archbishops of Canterbury, anointed him and placed upon his head 'a crown of pure gold adorned with precious stones'.

We catch, at this ceremony, a glimpse of the young king's mentality. He had just been anointed with holy oil, an act inspired by the anointing in the Old Testament of King Solomon by Zadok the priest. Henry asked one of the guests, Robert Grosseteste, a celebrated theologian who later became Bishop of Lincoln, what 'precise grace' was wrought in a king by this anointing. After pausing for thought, Grosseteste replied that it was 'the sign of the king's special reception of the sevenfold gifts of the Spirit, as in Confirmation'.

Henry was a pious king, attracted by theology rather than by war, and inclined to take a high view of the rights conferred on him by God. He made it his life's work to rebuild Westminster Abbey as a fitting church in which to house the shrine, adorned with 'purest gold and precious stones', of his predecessor, Edward the Confessor, who had reigned from 1042 to 1066 and was revered as the patron saint of England. The lofty building which we see today is described by Pevsner as 'the most French of all English Gothic churches', its roof supported by double tiers of flying buttresses. Henry spent £41,000 on this masterpiece, which made it the second most expensive building in medieval England, its cost exceeded only by Edward III's work at Windsor Castle. The interior of the abbey would have looked, when Henry built it, far richer and more highly coloured than it does now, the purity of its architecture uninterrupted by the jumble of monuments heaped up in more recent times. He deserves to be remembered as one of the great royal builders.

At the age of nineteen, Henry declared himself of age, and ready to govern, and a few years later he dispensed with the services of Hubert de Burgh. The king proceeded to spend so heavily that he brought himself to the brink of bankruptcy. When he was twenty-eight, he married Eleanor of Provence, who was fourteen. He showered such a wealth of gifts on her and her greedy relations that he became very unpopular, and so did she. These people were foreigners, and the English resented paying extortionate taxes in order to enable them to live in the lap of luxury. On one occasion, as Eleanor was rowed under London Bridge, she was pelted with mud and rubbish, and the mob shouted: 'Down with the witch! Let's drown her!'

Henry's mother, Isabella of Angoulême, returned home and married Hugh de Lusignan, to whom she had been betrothed before King John insisted on marrying her. She was young enough to have a second family, several of whom turned up at Henry's court and were likewise treated with excessive generosity. As the chronicler Matthew Paris put it, 'he exalted his uterine brothers [the Lusignans] in a most intolerable manner, contrary to the law of the kingdom as though they had been born in this country. Moreover, the king was reproached with advancing and enriching the interests of all foreigners, and with despising and pillaging his own natural subjects, to the ruin of the whole kingdom.'

Some lighter anecdotes survive from this time. In 1255, the King of France presented Henry with an elephant for the royal menagerie at the Tower of London: the first to reach this side of the Channel since AD 43, when the Roman emperor Claudius brought a war elephant to Colchester. Matthew Paris records that people flocked to see the elephant, which he drew for his chronicle. A special house was made for this exotic creature, which was fed on beef and red wine, but in 1257 it died, apparently after drinking too much wine.

Despite an expensive war, Henry failed to regain any of the continental possessions lost by his father. He and the Pope instead cooked up a scheme to take over Sicily, which came to nothing. In 1258, the king was so indebted that he called a Parliament: a term first used in 1236, to mean a meeting of the Great Council, an essentially feudal gathering of the most powerful barons and churchmen. The king demanded a subsidy in order to pay the costs of the Sicilian debacle, which entailed a large payment to the Pope.

The barons found this intolerable. They united under Simon de Montfort, a forceful nobleman of French extraction who had married the king's sister. Henry was made to agree to the Provisions of Oxford, which obliged him to submit to a council of twenty-four members, half chosen by himself and half by the barons, who would themselves choose two men to run the country. For the first time, this agreement was written down in English as well as in Latin and French. Two centuries after the Conquest, the English nation was beginning to emerge.

Henry soon managed, with the support of his ally, the Pope, to overthrow the agreement, and the result was civil war. In 1264, the barons led by de Montfort defeated the king at the Battle of Lewes, in Sussex, and captured both Henry and his twenty-four-year-old son and heir, Edward. The king was now powerless. De Montfort proceeded to widen his support by calling a Parliament to which were summoned for the first time knights of the shire and representatives of those towns friendly to him. Like many constitutional innovations, this only revealed its full significance later.

Edward, a leader as resolute as his father was feeble, now escaped by the clever expedient of suggesting a horse race to his captors, which he won, after which he galloped off into the distance. He rallied the royal forces, promised to uphold Magna Carta, and marched on de Montfort, who was forced, without having managed to assemble his full strength, to fight the Battle of Evesham. The rebels were surrounded and massacred: a bloody vengeance for their victory at Lewes. Henry, who was being held prisoner in the midst of the rebel army, was rescued. De Montfort's dead body was mutilated, his head, hands, feet and balls cut off.

Once the last remnants of the rebellion had been stamped out, the remainder of Henry III's reign passed peacefully. He was buried in Westminster Abbey, in a handsome tomb close to the shrine he had erected for Edward the Confessor, the saint after whom he had also named his eldest son.

EDWARD I

1272–1307

Edward I is one of the most formidable warrior kings of English history. He became known as the Hammer of the Scots, but actually conquered the Welsh. Before ascending the throne, he crushed the rebellion by the barons against his father, Henry III, and strengthened the grip on England of the royal administration.

When Edward heard he had become king, he was in Sicily, where he and his wife, Eleanor of Castile, were returning from the Crusade. They received, by successive messengers, two bad bits of news: first that their son and heir, Prince John, had died at the age of five, and then that the king had died. Their host asked why Edward received the first tidings with equanimity, but the second with inconsolable grief. The new king replied that while it was easy to have more sons, 'when a man has lost a good father, it is not in the course of nature for God to send him another'. The couple had at least fourteen children, most of whom died young.

Edward and Eleanor returned home in easy stages. He took part, with 1,000 English knights, in a tournament at Chalon, in Burgundy, which degenerated into an attempt to murder him. But Edward, who because of his great height was also known as Longshanks, fought off his assailants.

In August 1274, Edward and Eleanor landed at Dover and were soon after crowned, amid scenes of wild rejoicing, in the great new church of Westminster Abbey, erected by his father. For the first time since the Norman Conquest, the crown of Edward the Confessor was used at a coronation, and this for a king who bore the same name. A hundred knights who arrived as an escort for King Alexander III of Scotland allowed their horses to run free, and anyone who caught them could keep them. The profligacy of the Scottish knights was imitated by the English, who likewise loosed their horses. The feasting was on an unprecedented scale, and lasted a fortnight.

Edward and Eleanor had married in 1254, when she was only ten years old and he was fifteen: she lived at Windsor until she was old enough for the marriage to be consummated, whereupon they fell deeply in love with each other. Later writers claimed that when Edward was stabbed, while on crusade, by an assassin with a poisoned dagger, Eleanor saved his life by sucking out the poison.

Whether or not that is true, Edward declared in a letter written after she died at Harby, near Lincoln, in 1290: 'My harp is turned to mourning, in life I loved her dearly, nor can I cease to love her in death.' The king erected for her the most notable memorial to any English queen: the series of twelve Eleanor Crosses marking the places where her body lay overnight as it was carried in stages from Lincoln to London, where she was buried in Westminster Abbey. Three of these crosses survive, while a fourth, outside Charing Cross Station in London, is a copy erected some way from the original site in order to draw attention to the station hotel.

After a more than decent interval of nine years, Edward married Margaret of France. Despite the disparity in their ages – she was forty years younger than him – this too seems to have been a happy marriage, and she bore three children.

Llewellyn ap Gwynedd, Prince of Wales, refused either to attend Edward's coronation in 1274, or to do homage to him. Edward therefore conquered Llewellyn by rendering his safe retreat, the mountains of Snowdonia, uninhabitable. The king did this by building a chain of mighty castles, inspired by those he had seen on crusade, along the coast of North Wales, including Harlech, Caernarvon, Beaumaris and Conway, which cut the mountains off from Anglesey, Llewellyn's source of grain. Even today, these fortresses convey implacable determination.

Llewellyn saw his cause was hopeless, and in 1282 perished in battle. His brother, Daffydd, was hanged, drawn and quartered: the horrible new punishment invented for traitors. According to the *Lanercost Chronicle*, he

was first drawn [through the streets], then hanged as a thief; thirdly, he was beheaded alive, and his entrails burnt as an incendiary and homicide; fourthly, his limbs were cut into four parts as the penalty of a rebel, and exposed in four of the ceremonial places of England as a spectacle; to wit – the right arm with a ring on the finger in York; the left arm in Bristol; the right leg and hip at Northampton; the left [leg] at Hereford. But the villain's head was bound with iron, lest it should fall to pieces from putrefaction, and set conspicuously upon a long spear-shaft for the mockery of London.

It used to be said that Edward assured the Welsh they would now have a prince born in Wales, who spoke neither French nor English: and presented them on his shield with his infant son, Edward, born in Caernarvon Castle in 1284. But the title of Prince of Wales was actually conferred by the king on his heir at the Parliament which met in Lincoln in 1301.

While Edward was campaigning in Wales, one of his mounted knights was hit by an arrow fired from a longbow. This pierced the thick hauberk, or chain mail, protecting the knight's thigh, drove through the upper leg including the bone, penetrated the hauberk inside the thigh, forced its way through the wooden saddle and went deep into the horse. The English had not come across this fearsome weapon before, which was to make their armies almost invincible. Edward proceeded to deploy Welsh archers against the Scots.

But Scotland turned out to be a more complicated problem. He hoped at first for a peaceful solution: in 1286, Alexander III died, and was succeeded by his granddaughter Margaret, the Maid of Norway. Edward arranged for her to be brought to Scotland, where she was to marry his son, but unfortunately she died on the way, in the Orkney Islands. The Scots now asked him to adjudicate between several different candidates for the Scottish throne. Edward chose John Balliol, but proceeded to insult the Scots by treating him as a mere puppet.

Goaded beyond endurance, Balliol formed an alliance with France. This did him no good. In 1296, Edward stormed Berwick, and his forces crushed the Scots at the Battle of Dunbar. In the words of one observer, he 'conquered the Kingdom of Scotland and searched it through in twenty-one weeks'. Edward made a grand progress through the country, forced Balliol to abdicate, received the submission of many other notables and returned to London bearing the Stone of Scone, on which the kings of Scots were traditionally crowned.

And that, Edward thought, should have been that. But his high-handed behaviour provoked the creation of a resistance movement from which today's nationalists still draw inspiration. Its first leader was William Wallace, a giant warrior of iron strength who defeated the English at Stirling Bridge in 1297, was himself defeated the next year by Edward at Falkirk, but waged a guerrilla campaign until 1305, when he was captured, after which he too was hanged, drawn and quartered.

In order to raise money for the war on Scotland, Edward in 1295 summoned the Model Parliament: so called because it served as the model for later Parliaments. This had 400 representatives, more than de Montfort's Parliament of 1265. The king knew he needed the English nation on his side, and that he would be better off working through Parliament, whose members had the detailed local knowledge needed to help raise taxes. They were there to assist him, not to check him, and no one dreamed at this time of giving Parliament any role in making the laws: that was done by Edward himself.

The king was a celebrated legislator. By a statute of 1278, he demanded *quo warranto* – by what right – barons had set up their own courts without royal permission. If they could not give a satisfactory answer, their courts were abolished. By the Statute of Mortmain, he prevented tenants from leaving their property to the Church, a practice which was depriving landlords including himself of revenue. By the Statute of Acton Burnell, he helped merchants to recover debts, but he also imposed heavier customs duties on them. Edward attempted to standardise the acre at 4,840 square yards, but England was not yet prepared to accept such thoroughness, and wide variations continued to exist in different counties.

He behaved with great harshness towards the Jews, and in 1290 expelled them from England, after which he relied instead on Italian bankers for loans. Within his domestic circle, he had a tendency, like most of the Plantagenets, to lose his temper from time to time. A royal account book of 1297 includes the cost of repairing his daughter Elizabeth's coronet, which he had hurled into the fire.

He had a sense of justice, but not of any very modern kind. In 1303, while he was away hammering the Scots, his treasury at Westminster was broken into and all the Crown Jewels were stolen. The thieves were caught and their skins were nailed to the treasury door.

But Scotland still would not submit. Once Wallace had been put to death, a new leader of the resistance emerged, called Robert the Bruce. In 1306 Robert had himself crowned King of Scots, after which he spent much of his time in hiding.

During this period, according to Sir Walter Scott, 'an incident took place which, although it rests only on tradition in families of the name of Bruce, is rendered probable by the manners of the times'. Scott brought to an enthusiastic public the story of Bruce, close to despair, taking fresh courage from a spider, in the roof of the hovel where he had taken refuge, which failed six times to attach its thread to a neighbouring beam, but persevered and at the seventh attempt succeeded. According to Scott, 'I have often met with people of the name of Bruce, so completely persuaded of the truth of this story, that they would not on any account kill a spider.'

Edward knew Bruce would have to be suppressed, and set out in the summer of 1307 to deal with him. He instead fell ill, and in July, within sight of the Scottish border near Carlisle, he died. He had just had his sixty-eighth birthday: an exceptional age in medieval England, where men were generally reckoned to be growing old in their forties. His last order was that his son should carry his own bones at the head of the army until the Scots had been thoroughly and finally defeated.

EDWARD II

1307–1327

This hapless king refused to conform and came to a painful end. He was twenty-three when he ascended the throne, and soon abandoned the campaign against the Scots which his father had ordered him to pursue to a successful conclusion. For while Edward I, by being a great war leader, corresponded closely to the medieval ideal of what a monarch should be, Edward II had other interests. He was a strong, healthy, good-looking man, and an excellent horseman, but his recreations were not of a martial character. He loved music and was followed everywhere by minstrels. More worryingly, he was the only one of our medieval kings who knew how to swim. Today this is regarded as a wholesome form of exercise, but in 1307 it was seen as the spooky embrace of an unnatural element.

Some of his other recreations were likewise viewed with appalled incomprehension by the feudal hierarchy. Edward liked to mix with the common people and practise their skills. He learned thatching among the thatchers, horse-shoeing among the blacksmiths and at Christmas went rowing on the Fens with the wildfowlers.

Worse than any of that was the extreme partiality shown by Edward for a Gascon upstart called Piers Gaveston. Edward I had selected this boy as a companion for his son. Gaveston was amusing, handsome and impudent, and he and young Edward were soon passionately fond of each other. When the king took them campaigning in Scotland, the chroniclers compared them to David and Jonathan, the great biblical example of friendship between two young men.

In 1307, Edward asked his father to make Gaveston the Count of Ponthieu. The king flew into a rage and shouted: 'You baseborn whoreson! Do you want to give lands away now, you who never gained any?' He tore out a handful of Edward's hair and banished Piers. Edward responded by delaying the banishment and loading Piers with presents.

As soon as his father was dead, Edward II recalled Gaveston from exile and made him Earl of Cornwall, a title usually reserved for royalty. He kept a chamber for Gaveston close to his own, and married him to his niece, Margaret de Clare, the daughter of his sister Joan. And the following year, when the king went to Boulogne to get married to Isabella, the twelve-year-old daughter of Philip IV of France, he appointed Gaveston as regent in his absence.

These acts of favouritism to a foreigner seen as a nobody were more than a shock to the magnates of England: they were a mortal insult. The issue for the barons was not whether Gaveston was the king's lover, but the plain fact that he was being given honours, money and lands which they thought they ought to be getting themselves. On the day of the coronation, 25 February 1308, they told Edward, in the presence of Isabella, that they would boycott the ceremony unless he at once banished Gaveston. Edward mollified them by promising to obey the next Parliament.

The coronation went ahead, with Gaveston demonstrating a capacity for giving gratuitous offence which exceeds that of any other favourite in English history. He wore jewels which had just been presented to Edward by the King of France as part of Isabella's dowry. Gaveston, in imperial purple, was the most ostentatiously dressed man in Westminster Abbey. To him was given, by the king, not only the queen's jewellery, but the honour of carrying, on a velvet cushion, the sacred crown of St Edward the Confessor. And at the feast afterward, which Gaveston was supposed to be organising, the food arrived late, and was inedible. Queen Isabella wrote home to say how horrible the whole occasion had been.

Gaveston has exercised a fascination over ill-mannered, licentious youth which endures to this day. At Oxford University a society of dissolute or would-be dissolute undergraduates is named after him.

For the next three years, the barons made attempt after attempt to get rid of Gaveston. He responded by giving them rude nicknames: the Earl of Lincoln was Burst Belly, the Earl of Pembroke became Joseph the Jew and the Earl of Warwick the Black Dog of Arden. The Earl of Lancaster, who was emerging as the leader of the opposition, was the Fiddler.

In 1310, Edward was obliged to submit to a committee of the Lords Ordainers who imposed close restrictions on his powers, and said that Gaveston had 'misled and ill advised our lord the king and enticed him to do evil in various deceitful ways'. The next year, Gaveston was exiled to Flanders, but within two months he was back, and appeared at the king's Christmas court at Windsor. The Archbishop of Canterbury excommunicated Gaveston and preparations were made for civil war. Edward and Gaveston fled north, abandoning the pregnant Queen Isabella.

Early in 1312, Gaveston surrendered to the Earl of Pembroke with guarantees of safety, but the Earl of Lancaster seized him and had him beheaded beside the road from Warwick to Kenilworth. Four local cobblers sewed the head back on and presented the body to some nearby Dominican monks, an order favoured by the king.

Edward, stricken by Gaveston's murder, attempted to rebuild his authority by embarking on a campaign against the Scots. At the Battle of Bannockburn, in June 1314, his numerically superior army was routed by Robert the Bruce: a victory which assured the independence of Scotland for another 300 years.

The king now found in the Despensers, father and son, new favourites who became just as unpopular as Gaveston. Edward II was loyal to his friends, and they to him. The problem was that almost everyone else found his friends intolerable. The stubbornness which his father had demonstrated against the Welsh and the Scots was by Edward II directed against the English barons.

After many humiliations, Queen Isabella decamped to Paris with her lover, Roger Mortimer, making the excuse that 'someone has come between my husband and myself'. In 1326 she and Mortimer invaded England and placed themselves at the head of the opposition to Edward. They captured the Despensers, who were hanged, drawn and quartered.

Edward fled, but was handed over to Isabella by the Welsh. In January 1327, a group of twelve magnates confronted him in Kenilworth Castle, where he was being held, and demanded that he surrender the throne to his son, the future Edward III. Otherwise they would choose a new king, who was not a member of the royal family. Edward fainted, and fell on the floor 'as one dead', but on coming round, he left the room. He returned dressed in black, and handed over his crown, sceptre and other symbols of authority. For fear that his son would be disinherited, the king had consented to his own deposition. On 2 February 1327, Edward III was crowned king.

But Edward II was still alive. What was to be done with him? In April 1327 he was taken to Berkeley Castle. In July, he was rescued by a band of outlaws, but recaptured. In September, it was announced that he was dead. He was buried in Gloucester Abbey, where his tomb soon became a centre of pilgrimage.

And then the rumours of how he had met his end began to circulate. He is said to have been murdered by having six red-hot spits shoved up his arse. Kings' bodies were displayed after their death, in order to discourage foul play. Poisoning, strangulation and stabbing would all have left visible signs. But who would think of examining the royal rectum?

EDWARD III

1327–1377

Edward III ascended the throne at the age of fourteen in unfavourable circumstances. His father, Edward II, was in prison, and would nine months later be murdered. Power had been seized by the new king's mother, Isabella, and her lover, Roger Mortimer. The adulterous Isabella has become better known to history as the She-Wolf of France, with the poet Thomas Gray among those who blamed her for her husband's agonising death: 'She-Wolf of France, with unrelenting fangs, / That tear'st the bowels of thy mangled mate.'

During a Parliament held at Nottingham in the autumn of 1330, the young king and a band of companions entered the castle by a secret tunnel and captured the arrogant, unpopular Mortimer. Isabella pleaded for his life: 'Fair son, have pity on the gentle Mortimer.' But Edward had Mortimer taken to the Tower of London, accused of fourteen crimes including the murder of Edward II and usurping royal power, and hanged at Tyburn. Isabella was sent to live out her days at Castle Rising in Norfolk, where she led a luxurious existence until her death in 1358.

The overthrow of Mortimer was not the prelude to a reign of fear. Edward was adept at maintaining good relations with the barons, with Parliament and even, most unusually for a King of England, with his own family. He was married at the age of fifteen to Philippa of Hainault, who was a year older than him. They were devoted to each other and had fourteen children, of whom the most celebrated were their eldest son, the Black Prince, and their fourth son, John of Gaunt. These princes did not fall out with their parents and Philippa was a popular queen, known for her gentleness and charm: she persuaded Edward to spare the lives of the six burghers of Calais, who had surrendered the town to him after a long siege.

One means by which Edward bound the barons to him was by marrying his children to them. He encouraged the use of the English tongue: since 1066, the nobility had spoken French, but by 1350 they were also having English taught to their sons. Under Edward, the court stopped disdaining the local lingo. The first great writer of English, Geoffrey Chaucer, was born in about 1343, the son of a London vintner, and early in life found employment at court, where he married a lady-in-waiting to the queen and in 1374 received from the king exactly the encouragement an author needs, namely 'a gallon of wine daily for the rest of his life'.

But Edward found the best way of dissuading the barons from

making war at home, and fostering the growth of a national spirit, was to engage them in the more profitable pursuit of making war abroad. Froissart, the great chronicler of this period, observed that the English would never love or honour their king 'unless he be victorious and a lover of arms and war against their neighbours'. He also wrote, several centuries before there was any question of turning the country into a democracy: 'The King of England must needs obey his people and do all their will.'

The young king proceeded to fulfil, as his grandfather, Edward I, had done, the royal role of warlord. First he took revenge for Bannockburn: in 1333 the Scots were defeated at Halidon Hill. But campaigning in France offered the prospect of richer booty, and the French were in any case in alliance with the Scots.

Through his mother, the daughter of a French king, Edward in 1337 laid claim to the French throne. The French not surprisingly dismissed this claim: they pointed out that under Salic law their throne could not descend in the female line. To settle the matter, what became known as the Hundred Years War was fought.

In 1340 Edward won the naval battle of Sluys, which gave him command of the English Channel. On land, the longbow bestowed on the English a decisive advantage against heavily armed French knights. A skilled bowman could fire his sixth arrow before the first had landed: a devastating rate of fire. Boys supplied bundles of arrows in battle. The physical forces involved were so great that all trained archers developed twisted spines. Practice at the butts became the chief recreation in the villages of England: Edward prohibited under pain of imprisonment 'handball, football, or hockey; coursing and cockfighting, or other such idle games'.

The French nobility preferred to employ mercenary crossbowmen, recruited from Italy. They did not wish to supply their serfs with a deadly weapon which might be used in rebellion against themselves. But the heavier the armour a knight wore to protect himself, the more helpless he became once he was down, when he could be finished off by a man who inserted a knife into the joints between the armour.

In the summer of 1346, Edward plundered Normandy, sacked Caen and selected an excellent defensive position at Crécy, south of Calais, to meet the advancing French army. The French, who were numerically much superior, at once attacked, but then, in the words of Froissart, 'the English archers stepped forth one pace and let fly their arrows so wholly together and so thick that it seemed snow'. The French fought bravely but suffered a crushing defeat. Among those who fell on their side was the blind King of Bohemia, whose crest was three feathers and motto *Ich dien*, I serve: Edward's eldest son, the Black Prince, who at the age of sixteen had fought with distinction, took these for himself, and they are borne to this day by the Prince of Wales.

This destruction of the flower of French chivalry in no way precluded Edward from upholding chivalrous ideals. In 1348 he founded the Knights of the Garter, inspired by the legend of King Arthur, which remains England's highest order of chivalry. Here, amid much pomp and hierarchy, was an idea of equality: twenty-six knights sitting at a Round Table and bound, in the words of their historian, Elias Ashmole, writing in the seventeenth century, 'to be united in all Chances and various Turns of Fortune; copartners both in Peace and War; assistant to one another in all serious and dangerous exploits: and through the whole Course of their Lives to show Fidelity and Friendliness one towards another'.

But in 1348–9, England, in common with the rest of Europe, was afflicted by the Black Death, which carried off perhaps a third of the population. This terrible plague often returned, and is reflected in the art of the later Middle Ages, in which the Dance of Death and the Grim Reaper with his sickle are often found. In

1351, Parliament passed the Statute of Labourers, intended to hold down wages at a time when labourers were in short supply.

The thirst for war was scarcely abated by the plague. In 1356, the Black Prince won a great victory at Poitiers, about fifty miles south of the River Loire, at which he captured the French king, who was sent to England, where the King of Scots was already being held. In 1360, at the Treaty of Brétigny, peace was concluded: Edward's sovereignty over Calais and the whole of Aquitaine was recognised, and he in return abandoned his claim to the French throne.

From this high point, a rapid decline set in. The French set out to recover the lands they had lost. The Black Prince was ill, his brother John of Gaunt was a much less effective leader and Edward himself was sinking into his long dotage. After the death in 1369 of his beloved queen, he fell under the thumb of his mistress, Alice Perrers. In 1376, the Black Prince died, and so in the following year did Edward III.

RICHARD II

1377–1399

Richard II was only ten years old when he succeeded his grandfather, Edward III. Ceremonies inspired by chivalrous ideals had grown more elaborate over the past half-century, and for the first time the new king was conducted in a grand cavalcade from the Tower of London to Westminster, past allegorical tableaux and cheering crowds.

The conduits which supplied Londoners with water ran with wine. The boy king was dressed in white on a white charger, bareheaded beneath a canopy of blue velvet carried on silver poles by eight knights in armour. The next day he was given a grand coronation, at the end of which he fell asleep, and had to be carried out of Westminster Abbey by his tutor, Simon Burley.

This pageantry could not disguise the precariousness of his position. Richard's father, the Black Prince, was dead, but three of his uncles were still alive: the Duke of York, the Duke of Gloucester and, most worryingly, John of Gaunt, Duke of Lancaster, whose son, Henry Bolingbroke, was a year older than Richard. The two boys had been admitted earlier that year to the Order of the Garter by Edward III, on which occasion they had sworn not to take up arms against each other. But if Richard was to prove inadequate, the temptation to replace him would be irresistible.

The first challenge to Richard's authority came from a different quarter. In the first four years of his reign, the poll tax was levied, at the rate of a shilling a head and regardless of ability to pay, on no fewer than three occasions. People were fed up with paying, and in such an unfair way, for generally unsuccessful campaigns in France, and in 1381 they rose up in the Peasants' Revolt.

Rebels marched on London from Kent under the leadership of Wat Tyler, and also from Essex and Hertfordshire. They possessed a touching confidence that the king could right their wrongs, so their first demand was that they be allowed to talk to him. He said he would meet the Kentish peasants at Blackheath, and sailed down the Thames to them, but seeing how numerous they were, declined to land. The Mayor of London shut the gates against them, but rebel Londoners opened them again. John of Gaunt's magnificent Savoy Palace was smashed to pieces and burned to the ground, for he was blamed for the hated poll tax, and royal ministers, bishops and peers who were captured were killed.

Richard rode out from the Tower and met the rebels at Mile End. They demanded the handing over of 'traitors', an amnesty for themselves and emancipation from serfdom and labour service. The king agreed to these demands, and set his seal to the agreement. Participants in the uprising meanwhile broke into the Tower, where they caught the Archbishop of Canterbury as he tried to escape, and executed him. Several of them alarmed the king's mother, 'the Fair Maid of Kent', by asking her for a kiss.

The king held a second meeting with the rebels at Smithfield. Here Wat Tyler, who may have been drunk, grew abusive and was killed by the Mayor of London, William Walworth. Tyler's supporters made ready to fight, by stringing their bows. But the king rode towards them and said, 'Sirs, will you kill your king? I am your king, I your captain and your leader. Follow me into the fields.' And follow him they did.

It was generally recognised that the fourteen-year-old king had shown great courage during this crisis. But he soon reneged on the promises he had made to the rebels, and the lesson he may have drawn from the episode was that in defence of his prerogatives, any deceit was justified. In the following year, he married Anne of Bohemia, who brought to England the custom of ladies riding side-saddle. Their marriage was contented but childless.

Richard's leadership of the country was less happy. He was astonishingly extravagant: he built the great hammer-beam roof of Westminster Hall, which survives to this day and which most people will say was worth every penny. But to confer a pension of £1,000 a year on Leon V, an unhappy man who had been driven out of the kingdom of Armenia, was altogether more questionable. Since Richard had no taste or capacity for war, he could not keep the barons in order by leading them on successful campaigns. He instead lavished enormous gifts on favourites, notably Robert de Vere, and displayed a sublime faith in his own rights. The

Wonderful Parliament of 1386 tried to make him dismiss his cronies, but provoked the reply that at their behest he would not dismiss so much as a kitchen scullion.

For a long time Richard was strong enough to outwit his enemies, but not to dominate them. In 1387, they defeated him at the Battle of Radcot Bridge, after which the Merciless Parliament, led by the five Lords Appellant, imposed close restrictions on him and had several of his closest friends killed. Once again Richard wriggled free. He recruited a private army which wore his badge, the white hart. In the Wilton Diptych, the famous picture in the National Gallery of Richard II kneeling in front of the Virgin and Child, both he and the angels are wearing the white hart.

Richard reigned with a degree of restraint until his wife died in 1394, after which he became intolerably tyrannical. His second wife, Isabella of France, was in no position to restrain him, for in 1396, when they got married, she was only six years old.

Now no magnate felt secure: Richard might seize anyone's lands. In 1397, he struck against his enemies, including his uncle, the Duke of Gloucester, who was taken to Calais and strangled. He told his cousin, Henry Bolingbroke, that he must submit to trial by combat against another of his enemies, Thomas Mowbray; then at the last moment commuted this sentence to banishment.

In February 1399, Richard's uncle, John of Gaunt, died, and he confiscated his vast estates, which should have passed to Bolingbroke. But the king was now very clearly overplaying his hand. He departed for Ireland, to put down a rebellion there. Bolingbroke took advantage of his absence to sail from Boulogne to Yorkshire. As soon as he landed, discontented barons flocked to join him. Richard returned from Ireland to North Wales, where he had once enjoyed strong support, but he was betrayed into Bolingbroke's hands.

Bolingbroke seized the throne, and Richard was incarcerated

first in the Tower of London and then in Pontefract. Here his dungeon was filled with rotting meat, but his constitution was so strong that he survived this attempt at germ warfare. He was therefore, as far as we can tell, starved to death. His high idea of kingship, according to which he was entitled to do whatever he pleased with his God-given powers regardless of anyone else's view, had proved fatal to him.

HENRY IV

1399–1413

Henry Bolingbroke was a usurper. In July 1399, when he returned to England from banishment in France, so many barons rallied to his side that he realised he was in a position, not merely to enforce his rights, but to exceed them. So he imprisoned Richard II, summoned a Parliament to meet in Westminster Hall, had the king's abdication and a long list of his crimes read out, and claimed the English throne for himself.

By what right did Bolingbroke do this? He himself seems to have been troubled by this question, to which there was no satisfactory answer. Richard, the lawfully anointed king, was still alive, and his heir, since he had no children, was Edward Mortimer, Earl of March, who was seven years old. Mortimer was descended from Lionel of Antwerp, Duke of Clarence, who was Edward III's third son. Bolingbroke himself was the son of John of Gaunt, Duke of Lancaster, who was a considerable figure, but was Edward III's fourth son.

Bolingbroke, born in 1366, was the first Plantagenet from the House of Lancaster to ascend the throne, and could claim to be a major figure in his own right: a warrior known throughout Christendom, rather than a mere boy. He had campaigned with the Teutonic Knights in Prussia, and had made a grand journey to Jerusalem, going out by way of Prague, Vienna, Venice, Corfu and Rhodes, and returning via Cyprus, Rhodes, Venice, Milan and Paris. At the age of fourteen he had married an heiress, Mary de Bohun, who died after giving birth to their seventh child.

The question of legitimacy mattered, for it had a direct bearing on how ready his temporary coalition of barons would feel in the future to rebel. So the new king had an even bigger and better coronation than his predecessor, during which he received an astonishing mark of divine favour: the oil with which he was anointed was said to have been given in a golden chalice by the Virgin Mary to Thomas à Becket, the greatest saint of medieval England. She promised Thomas that the first king to be anointed with this oil would perform great deeds, including the recovery of Normandy and Aquitaine. It was said that the oil had been kept hidden, but had recently been rediscovered.

Not everyone was impressed by the story of the oil: one chronicler reported that when it was poured on Henry's head, the lice ran out. Early the next year, Richard was put to death in Pontefract, after the discovery of the first plot against Henry's life, led by three earls the new king had demoted. He responded with a ferocity inspired by fear: thirty rebels were executed.

Henry was anxious for the support of the Church and in 1401 the law *De heretico comburendo* appeared on the statute book, permitting for the first time in England the burning of heretics at the stake. The Church was determined to extirpate the Lollards, the followers of John Wycliffe, a theologian who attacked the papacy, translated the Bible into English, and became known as 'the morning star of the Reformation'.

But resistance to Henry spread. The Welsh rose under Owen Glendower, who in 1403 formed a most menacing alliance with the Earl of Northumberland and his son, Harry Hotspur. We enter Shakespearean territory: eight of his history plays are set in the period of just over eighty years from this rebellion against Henry IV to the death in battle of Richard III at Bosworth Field. Shakespeare's Henry IV says with truth: 'Uneasy lies the head that wears a crown.'

Henry and his son, the future Henry V, won the Battle of Shrewsbury, a bloody conflict in which Hotspur was killed. But the country was not at peace. Northumberland fomented an uprising in the north, which was joined by Richard Scrope, Archbishop of York, who denounced Henry for usurping the throne, murdering Richard II and levying unjust taxes.

This insurrection also failed, and Henry commanded the Chief Justice, Sir William Gascoigne, to sentence the archbishop to death. Gascoigne refused, pointing out that Scrope was entitled to judgement by his peers. Henry nevertheless secured, with the help of a more pliant lawyer, the archbishop's execution: an act which was not just deeply unpopular, but was said to have precipitated, as a sign of God's displeasure, the painful disease, described as leprosy, from which Henry suffered until his death. His face and body were disfigured, and he became a recluse, but he drew comfort from a prophecy that he would die in Jerusalem.

In March 1413, the king suffered a stroke while praying at the shrine of Edward the Confessor in Westminster Abbey. He was taken to the Jerusalem Chamber, in the abbot's lodgings. On being told where he was, he said: 'Now I know that I shall die here in this chamber.' And so he did.

HENRY V

1413–1422

By defeating the French, Henry V united the English. He was the last great warrior king of the Middle Ages, and Shakespeare drew an immortal picture of him as a leader who on the way to victory at Agincourt inspired his followers not just by his courage, but by mingling with them in the dark hours before the battle. Here is English patriotism in its most cheerful form: 'We few, we happy few, we band of brothers.' If you want to see what I mean, watch Laurence Olivier, Richard Burton or Kenneth Branagh deliver the speech on YouTube.

But historians tend to draw Henry as a less sympathetic figure, who looked and behaved more like a monk than a happy-go-lucky first among equals. They observe that as king, he was intensely pious, and even before he was crowned, had presided at the burning of heretics. One of these Lollards, a tailor, cried out for mercy as the flames reached him. Henry had the fire put out, and urged the tailor to recant. When the man refused to do so, Henry had the fire relit. Here was a leader who insisted on being obeyed.

Some writers even cast doubt on Shakespeare's portrait of the young prince as a boon companion who only repudiated his drinking buddies on becoming king. Osbert Lancaster contends that since most of his time as Prince of Wales was spent fighting, 'with an efficiency that was universally acknowledged by his contemporaries', on the Welsh border, 'his acquaintance with the night life of the capital must necessarily have been slight and occasional'.

Henry had certainly undergone, while fighting the Welsh leader Owen Glendower, a military apprenticeship in which he revealed his gift for mobile warfare. At the Battle of Shrewsbury in 1403, when at the age of sixteen he was wounded in the face by an arrow but kept fighting, he had helped his father, Henry IV, to a decisive victory over the rebels. From 1406, there were rumours he was anxious to take over from his father, who was increasingly incapacitated by illness. It was said that when his father lay dying, he had actually tried on the crown.

From the start of his reign, Henry V did all he could to unite the nation behind his great design for war with France. He went out of his way to be reconciled with nobles who had been out of favour during the previous reign. Even more conspicuously, he arranged for the man his father had deposed and killed, Richard II, to be buried with full honours in the tomb that monarch had prepared for himself in Westminster Abbey.

France at this time was rent by civil war between two factions, the Burgundians and the Armagnacs. Henry V took care to keep them on bad terms with each other. He made an alliance with the Burgundians, and demanded from the Armagnacs the return of everything King John had managed to lose from the enormous continental possessions held by Henry II: a demand no French negotiator could accept.

So in August 1415, Henry set sail from Southampton, landed in Normandy and besieged Harfleur, which fell to him after a month, but not before many of his men had succumbed to disease. He now decided to march to Calais, which remained in English hands. At Agincourt, the larger French army which had been shadowing his tired, hungry and dysentery-ridden force blocked his way.

Henry, with characteristic prudence, tried to talk his way out of trouble: he even offered to return Harfleur. But the enemy, scenting victory, would have none of it. The flower of the French nobility advanced on foot into a funnel of narrow ground between two woods, where their superior numbers could not tell and they had no hope of outflanking the English. Knights pressing forward from behind denied those in front the space even to wield their weapons. Once one of these heavily armoured Frenchmen was down, stuck in the mud of the recently ploughed field, he had little chance of getting to his feet again.

The English archers, posted by Henry to one side and protected by sharpened stakes, inflicted terrible casualties before closing to finish off the wounded. Henry himself fought with conspicuous valour and ruthlessness: at a tense moment he ordered the slaughter of prisoners. By the end of the battle, about 6,000 of the French lay dead, including the pride of their chivalry, compared to 400 of the English.

The king returned in triumph to London. The French would

not risk a second pitched battle against him, so in another, much longer campaign he besieged and captured their towns one by one. In 1420, at the Treaty of Troyes, the Burgundians agreed that he would succeed to the French throne on the death of the aged and infirm Charles VI, and would meanwhile act as regent. The unfortunate Charles was subject to periodic bouts of madness during which he supposed he was made of glass, and forbade the approach of courtiers for fear of breaking him. Henry married Charles's daughter, the nineteen-year-old Catherine of Valois, at Troyes, and in December entered Paris with her.

He had achieved the astonishing feat of combining the English and French crowns, and brought Catherine to London, where in February 1421 she was crowned Queen of England in Westminster Abbey. But part of the deal with the Burgundians was that he would continue to campaign against Charles's French heir, the dauphin, who had incurred their undying hatred by having the previous Duke of Burgundy murdered. The dauphin still held France south of the Loire. Henry began his campaign against him by investing Meaux, the dauphin's last stronghold north of that river.

The town duly fell in May 1422, but Henry's luck had run out. During the siege, he had fallen ill, probably with dysentery, and in August he died at Bois de Vincennes, just outside Paris, at the age of thirty-four. So we shall never know what success this mighty king would have had in consolidating his enormous conquests. As he lay dying, he did not summon his young wife, Catherine, to his side, but calmly made arrangements for the regency which must follow while their newborn son grew up. Catherine some years later married and had several children with a Welshman, Owen Tudor, whose family was not yet of any significance.

HENRY VI

1422–1461

enry VI was one of the least successful kings in English history. He was also the youngest: only nine months old at the death of his father, Henry V. At the age of one year he appeared at public functions and took his place in Parliament. He was knighted at the age of four, and at the age of seven he was crowned in Westminster Abbey, when he was observed to look around him 'sadly and wisely'. The crown was too big and heavy for him, and had to be held on each side by two bishops.

For the rest of his life, the crown remained too heavy for Henry, and the barons who competed to help him carry it fell instead to slaughtering each other. Henry's desire was to spend his life meekly kneeling upon his knees. He was a man of spiritual seriousness who detested violence, longed for peace and found fulfilment as a patron of learning: he founded Eton College and King's College, Cambridge. Unlike every other king since the Norman Conquest, he never led his followers into battle. He would not and could not carry out his duties as a war leader, so left a vacuum which others tried to fill.

But at first all was well. His father's prestige meant there was no challenge in England to the infant ruler. Charles VI of France died two months later, so Henry was now king of both countries. His uncle, the Duke of Bedford, a man of great military ability, was charged with maintaining English rule in France, and did so with success until 1429.

That year saw the emergence of one of the strangest figures ever to blaze across the skies of Europe. Joan of Arc was a peasant girl who had heard the voices of three saints calling on her to save France. She appeared in a suit of white armour at the siege of Orleans, put new heart into the dispirited French defenders and forced the English to retreat. Joan followed up this success by marching with the dauphin through English-held territory to Reims, where by tradition the kings of France were crowned, and having him enthroned as Charles VII.

Bedford saw it was time for Henry to be crowned King of France, so in 1430 the nine-year-old boy was taken across the Channel. Joan had meanwhile fallen into the hands of the English, who passed her to their Burgundian allies, who had her burned as a witch. Henry's coronation as Henri II did not take place until December 1431. It was held in Notre Dame, in Paris, which was not the right place, and the French clergy were furious at being shut out of the affair. Henry's uncle, Cardinal Beaufort, Bishop of Winchester, placed the crown upon his head. The people of Paris broke into the hall where the coronation feast was to take place, and stole much of the food and drink.

The English were starting to lose all they had so recently conquered. Bedford died in 1435, and was succeeded by less able commanders. The Burgundians, whose support was indispensable, changed sides. In 1445, Henry married Margaret of Anjou, daughter of René of Anjou and a cousin of the French queen. He was twenty-four and his wife was fifteen, but she soon emerged as the more powerful personality.

By 1451, everything in France except Calais had gone. Even Gascony, in English hands for three centuries, had been lost after a final smashing defeat. In 1453, the Hundred Years War, which had actually lasted, with intermissions, for a bit more than a hundred years, came to an end with the Peace of Chatillon. The English were left with nothing to show for their exertions.

The peace-loving king may have hoped he would now get some peace. But in 1453 he suffered his first bout of madness: a condition probably inherited from his mad French grandfather, Charles VI. Henry fell into a catatonic state, could no longer speak, and did not react when his newborn son, Prince Edward, was presented to him. The Duke of York, who was next in line to the throne after this child, reigned as Protector. But then the king recovered his wits, such as they were, whereupon York was sacked and power was gathered into the hands of the Duke of Somerset and Queen Margaret.

In Shakespeare's version of events, the dukes of York and Somerset were walking one day with some other barons in the Temple gardens in London. York, who had failed to persuade any member of the company to voice support for him, instead plucked a white rose from a bush, stuck it in his cap and invited those who were on his side to do likewise. But Somerset plucked a red rose, after which the barons either picked red, to show that they were Lancastrians who supported the king, or white, to show they backed the Duke of York.

At the end of the Hundred Years War, many men who knew no trade but war returned from France and joined the private armies of various overmighty subjects. The Wars of the Roses broke out: a period of intermittent civil war during which the English nobility slew each other.

The Duke of York was at first victorious: in 1455 he killed Somerset at the Battle of St Albans. It was decided that York would once more rule the country as Protector, and become king when Henry died. But Henry's wife, Margarèt, was not prepared to accept the disinheriting of their only child, Prince Edward. In 1460, York went so far as to claim the throne, but was defeated and killed at the Battle of Wakefield, after which his head, wearing a paper crown, was displayed on the gates of York.

Early in 1461, Margaret managed, at the second Battle of St Albans, to rescue her husband from the Yorkists. Henry had again gone mad: sitting under a tree, he laughed and sang during the battle. And despite this victory, London shut its gates against Margaret, fearful of being pillaged by her rough northern troops. The Lancastrians could not prevent York's son, Edward, entering the capital with the help of Richard Neville, Earl of Warwick, known to history as Warwick the Kingmaker. Nothing now stood between the Yorkists and the throne.

EDWARD IV
1461–1483

U nlike the man he had driven off the throne, Edward IV looked and behaved like a king. The head of the House of York was tall, athletic and good-looking: a French chronicler described him as 'the handsomest prince my eyes ever beheld'. And, although only nineteen years old, he possessed great military ability. In March 1461, after his proclamation in London as king, he pursued the Lancastrians to Yorkshire and cut them to pieces in a snowstorm at Towton, probably the bloodiest battle ever fought on English soil. Henry and Margaret fled to Scotland, while Edward returned to London and was crowned amid scenes of popular enthusiasm.

Warwick the Kingmaker, whose help had proved essential, was richly rewarded for his services. He and his brothers continued to mop up Lancastrian resistance in the north of England, which continued until 1464. Henry, the deposed king, was captured in 1465, after spending a year on the run, and was imprisoned in the Tower of London. Here he composed a poem in which he remarked, 'Kingdoms are but cares'.

Warwick meanwhile pursued an ambitious programme of diplomacy with the French court, which he expected to result in the grant of lands in France to himself as well as marriage between Edward and a French princess. So it came as a shock to Warwick to discover in 1464 that his protégé had instead married, in secret, an English commoner. She was Elizabeth Woodville, a beautiful young widow with two children by her first husband, a knight who had died fighting on the Lancastrian side.

Edward was an insatiable womaniser: it was said of him that 'he pursued with no discrimination the married and the unmarried, the noble and lowly'. Woodville was said to have lain in wait for him behind an oak tree while the king was hunting in Whittlebury Forest, in Northamptonshire. Stepping in front of him, she pleaded for the return of her husband's property. When Edward, captivated by her beauty, tried to seduce her, she replied: 'My liege, I know I am not good enough to be your queen, but I am far too good to be your mistress.' So the ardent young king married her.

This action antagonised not just Warwick but most of the English nobility. Woodville added insult to injury by bringing with her, as queens so often did, a plethora of poor relations, who were rewarded with rich marriages of their own. And Edward further defied Warwick by favouring an alliance with Burgundy instead of France.

Warwick reckoned that if Edward would not do his bidding,

it was time to change the king. He at first attempted to install the king's brother, the Duke of Clarence, on the throne. After that manoeuvre failed, he fell back on Henry VI, who was still imprisoned in the Tower, where according to his confessor, John Blacman, 'like a true follower of Christ, he patiently endured hunger, thirst, mockings, derisions, abuse and many other hardships'. In the summer of 1470, Warwick took Edward by surprise, forced him to flee to the continent, and installed Henry as king: the so-called Readeption. In the words of a chronicler, during this manoeuvre Henry 'was as mute as a crowned calf'.

Edward returned in March 1471 at the head of a small force. He landed in Yorkshire and, gathering adherents on his march south, arrived at Barnet, north of London, where he defeated and killed Warwick, after which he defeated Warwick's ally, Margaret, who had arrived too late with a second army. In this second engagement, at Tewkesbury, Margaret and Henry's son, Edward, was slain. On the night Edward IV returned to London, Henry himself was murdered in the Tower: an event remembered each year by the provosts of Eton and King's College, Cambridge, the two great institutions founded by that pious but luckless king.

The Lancastrian claimants to the throne were now all dead, except for Henry Tudor, who lived in exile and whose claim was remote. Edward faced no more challenges to his authority. His brother, the Duke of Clarence, who had dabbled in treason with Warwick, had returned to the king's side. In 1478, when Clarence showed signs of dabbling once more in treachery, Edward inflicted on him one of the most memorable deaths in English history: he was drowned in a butt of malmsey wine.

Edward took the chance, during the second half of his reign, to sort out the royal finances. His three Lancastrian predecessors were always short of money, but he left the royal treasury full, promoted the wool trade and suppressed the brigandage which had flourished during the civil war. He threatened to invade France, but allowed himself to be bought off by a pension from the French king.

For the rest, he indulged his appetites for food and women. Many of the women were the wives and daughters of rich merchants in the City of London: Edward was no snob and had a healthy interest in money. He also became a friend and patron of William Caxton, who introduced printing into England. But in April 1483 the king went fishing on the Thames, caught what sounds like pneumonia and died unexpectedly at the age of forty.

EDWARD V

1483

According to the Bristol Calender for 1483, 'In this year, the two sons of King Edward were put to silence in the Tower.' After more than six centuries, the bare record, compiled by an official in that city, still strikes a chill. The princes entered the Tower and were put to silence. Their uncle, younger brother of their father, had himself crowned as Richard III. The overwhelming likelihood is that he did what usurpers usually did if they could, in this period of our history, to rivals with better claims to the throne. He had them murdered.

A number of enthusiasts deny that this is almost certainly what happened, and prefer to treat these events as if they occurred in a detective story by Agatha Christie set in the early twentieth century, where the prime suspect never turns out to be the murderer. The implausibility of such an approach will be seen both in this life of Edward V, whose reign of seventy-eight days was the shortest for an English monarch, and in the account which follows of Richard III.

On 9 April 1483, when Edward IV died at Westminster, his heir, Edward, Prince of Wales, was staying with his mother at Ludlow, close to the Welsh border. The queen and the rest of the Woodville family feared that Edward IV's younger brother, Richard, Duke of Gloucester, who had been named as Protector during the new king's minority, would try to seize power. They were also afraid he would take revenge for the death of the Duke of Clarence: the royal brother put to death by Edward IV with the encouragement of the queen.

The Woodvilles tried to pre-empt Richard by having Edward V taken as quickly as possible to London and crowned. The new king set out from Ludlow with his maternal uncle, Lord Rivers, and an escort of 2,000 men. Richard hastened south from York and intercepted Edward V at Stony Stratford, the town near Northampton where Watling Street crosses the Great Ouse. The Duke of Buckingham, another opponent of the Woodvilles, helped Richard to arrest Lord Rivers, who was conducted north and executed, and to take control of the king.

Edward was brought to London by the Protector, who set about dispossessing him of the throne. The queen found sanctuary at Westminster Abbey with her younger son, Richard, Duke of York, who was ten. But she was at length prevailed upon to part with him too, every promise being made to her that he would be safe.

The two boys were housed in the Tower of London, where it was traditional for the next king to stay for a few days before being taken in a grand procession to Westminster for coronation. Meanwhile their uncle arranged for himself to be crowned. Dominic Mancini, an Italian who visited England in 1483, described to the best of his ability what happened next:

> Edward V and his brother were withdrawn into the inner apartments of the Tower proper and day by day began to be seen more rarely until at length they ceased to appear altogether. A Strasbourg doctor, the last of his attendants whose service the king enjoyed, reported that the young king like a victim prepared for sacrifice sought remission for his sins through daily confession and penance, because he believed that death was facing him. Already there was a suspicion that he had been done away with, and by what manner of death so far I have not at all discovered.

By the end of 1483 it was widely believed that the princes must have been murdered. As the author of the *Croyland Chronicle* wrote: 'A rumour was spread that the sons of King Edward had died a violent death, but it was uncertain how.'

Thirty years later, Thomas More wrote his *History of Richard III*, which gives a detailed account of how the princes died. Richard entrusted the task to an ambitious man called Tyrell, for whom he obtained admission to the Tower:

> Sir James Tyrell devised that they should be murdered in their beds. To the execution whereof, he appointed Miles Forest, one of the four that kept them, a fellow hardened in murder before that time. To him he joined one John Dighton, his own housekeeper, a big, broad, square strong knave. Then all the others being removed from them, this Miles Forest and John Dighton about midnight (the innocent chil-

dren lying in their beds) came into the chamber, and suddenly lapped them up among the bedclothes – so bewrapped them and entangled them, keeping down by force the featherbed and pillows hard unto their mouths, that within a while, smothered and stifled, their breath failing, they gave up to God their innocent souls into the joys of heaven, leaving to the tormentors their bodies dead in the bed. Which after that the wretches perceived, first by the struggling with the pains of death, and after long lying still, to be thoroughly dead, they laid their bodies naked out upon the bed, and fetched Sir James to see them. Who, upon the sight of them, caused those murderers to bury them at the stair-foot, suitably deep in the ground, under a great heap of stones.

In 1674, workmen demolishing a staircase at the Tower of London came upon a wooden chest containing the skeletons of two children. These were quite reasonably assumed to be the remains of the princes, and on Charles II's orders they were reburied in Westminster Abbey. In 1933, tests on the bones showed them to be of children aged about twelve and ten.

Such striking confirmation of one part of More's account has not deterred supporters of Richard III from dismissing it as 'Tudor propaganda': a fantasy with as little foundation in fact as his famous work Utopia. But More was a man of high principle who lost his life because he had the courage to defy Henry VIII. To dismiss him and Shakespeare as mere propagandists is unfair.

The fascinating question of whether Richard ordered the murder of Edward V should not be allowed to obscure the truth that he seized control of the two heirs to the throne, the sons of his older brother, and had them confined to the Tower of London, after which they disappeared.

RICHARD III

1483–1485

R ichard III arouses stronger feelings than any other English king. His defenders protest that he is the victim of an atrocious miscarriage of justice, and complain that he has been defamed, most devastatingly by Shakespeare, as a poisonous hunchbacked toad and a child-murderer.

Horace Walpole began, in the eighteenth century, the fashion for suggesting that Richard III was not so bad as Shakespeare had painted him. Walpole contended that 'the crimes of Richard, which he really committed, at least which we have reason to believe he committed, were more the crimes of the age than the man': a fair enough point. It was at this time the custom for a king to kill, if he got the chance, anyone who threatened him.

But like the more recent defenders of Richard, Walpole cannot resist plunging into a detailed and enjoyable examination of the evidence, during which he makes a host of astute observations on particular points, and also convinces himself that Richard is almost entirely innocent. These advocates exaggerate the case in the king's favour at least as much as they accuse others of exaggerating the case against.

Richard was born in 1452, the youngest of the ten children of the Duke of York. Three years later, the Wars of the Roses broke out, with the Duke of York contending for the throne against the Lancastrians, whose figurehead was Henry VI. In 1460 the duke and one of his sons were killed at the Battle of Wakefield, and Richard was taken to the Low Countries for his own safety. But the following year, the new Duke of York, Richard's older brother Edward, gained decisive victories over the Lancastrians with the help of Warwick the Kingmaker, and installed himself as Edward IV.

Richard, who was still only eight years old, spent the next four years as a henchman, or apprentice knight, in the household of Warwick the Kingmaker. In 1466, he attended a feast to celebrate the enthronement of Warwick's brother as Archbishop of York: it was prepared by sixty-two cooks and included a hundred oxen, six bulls, 4,000 sheep, 500 stags and 400 swans, 75,000 gallons of ale and 25,000 gallons of wine.

In 1469, at the age of seventeen, Richard commanded the

troops who regained Carmarthen and Cardigan from rebels. Two years later, when Warwick the Kingmaker rebelled against Edward IV, Richard remained loyal to the king, and was almost captured with him at Doncaster as they fled to the Low Countries, where they stayed with Charles the Bold, Duke of Burgundy, who had married one of their sisters.

Edward and Richard soon returned to England, and won decisive victories in which Richard played a major part. Edward sent Richard to govern the north of England, which he did with exemplary loyalty and efficiency, even winning Berwick-upon-Tweed back from the Scots. So in the spring of 1483, during the king's last illness, it was natural for him to entrust his son and heir, Edward, to Richard as Protector.

At first, it seemed Richard would respect this arrangement. He swore an oath of fealty to Prince Edward. But he also moved south from York and intercepted the prince, who was being taken to London for coronation. The two kinsmen of Edward IV's queen who were accompanying the prince were arrested, taken north to Pontefract, and executed. Richard and his ally, the Duke of Buckingham, continued to London with the prince. The initiative lay with Richard, who summoned his loyal followers from Yorkshire to 'come unto us to London . . . with as many as ye can make defensibly arrayed, there to aid and assist us against the queen, her bloody adherents and affinity'.

Richard started to take soundings about getting himself crowned. Lord Hastings raised objections at a meeting of the Council, so was taken outside, where his head was laid on a log of timber and struck off. The claim was put about that Edward IV's marriage had been invalid, so his sons were unable to inherit the throne.

A clergyman was found to preach on the text 'Bastard slips shall not take root', and Parliament was prevailed upon to pass an Act, *Titulus Regius*, which stated that Edward V and his brother were illegitimate. The two princes were confined to the Tower, and no more was heard of them. On 6 July 1483, Richard and his wife, Anne, walked barefoot to Westminster Abbey and were crowned in a magnificent ceremony.

But throughout these events, no sign of popular enthusiasm for Richard could be detected. It was one thing for him to seize the crown; quite another to hold it. He rewarded his chief supporters with grants of land, and set off on a royal progress through the north, the only part of his kingdom where people were at all fond of him. But almost at once he received news of a menacing new combination. The Duke of Buckingham, who had helped to put him on the throne, now conspired to throw him off it again, and was in league not only with the Woodvilles but with Henry Tudor, the surviving Lancastrian claimant, who was planning an invasion from France.

Luckily for Richard, Henry's fleet was scattered by a storm, and Buckingham's forces also melted away under the impact of heavy rain. The new king captured Buckingham without a fight and had him executed. Richard could assure himself that all might yet be well. He set out to win his people's confidence by getting Parliament to pass just laws. Juries were to be free from pressure, bail would be granted to arrested men and the double selling of property was prohibited. The king also renounced the raising of forced loans, known as benevolences: but then reinstated them, because he must have money for defence.

The following year, Richard suffered an irreparable blow. In April 1484, his only son, Prince Edward, died at the age of ten. According to one chronicler, 'you might have seen his father and mother in a state almost bordering on madness by reason of their sudden grief'. It was now far less likely Richard's line would continue, so far less tempting to be loyal to him. Just under a year later, Anne died too. There were horrible rumours that he had poisoned her in order to bolster his position by marrying his niece, Elizabeth of York.

The king was isolated. He had failed to win the allegiance, much less the love, of either the nobility or the people. He did not inspire loyalty, and ruled with the help of a few men he had known since they were boys. A malicious rhyme circulated:

> The Cat, the Rat
> And Lovell our Dog
> Rulen all England
> Under an Hog.

The Hog was Richard, whose symbol was a blue boar, while the Cat, the Rat and the Dog were William Catesby, Sir Richard Ratcliffe and Francis Lovell.

In August 1485, Henry Tudor landed at Milford Haven with 2,000 French soldiers, who were joined by 3,000 men from Wales and Shropshire. Henry held talks with Lord Stanley, whose son was being held hostage by Richard.

The king still managed to raise 10,000 men. On 20 August, he reviewed them at Leicester. The Battle of Bosworth Field, which followed, should have been a victory for Richard. He was a seasoned warrior with a superior army deployed on an elevated position.

But early in the battle, the commander of the vanguard, the Duke of Norfolk, was killed, and his followers fled. Nor would the king's rearguard, commanded by the Earl of Northumberland, come forward. The Stanley brothers, who had substantial forces of their own, stood by and watched how the fighting would go. They could be presumed to be favourable to Henry, whose mother, Margaret, was now married to Lord Stanley: but Richard had taken the precaution of holding Stanley's son, Lord Strange, as a hostage.

The king's fatal weakness was that almost no one really wanted to fight for him. He attempted to settle the issue himself by mounting with only about eighty men a direct attack on Henry Tudor, who was at the rear of the battlefield. Richard cut down Henry's standard-bearer and almost reached Henry himself, but was surrounded by the Stanleys, who now committed their men with decisive effect. The king, fighting with desperate bravery, was killed. His crown rolled under a hawthorn bush and is said to have been retrieved by Lord Stanley, who placed it on Henry's head.

Richard's corpse was stripped and flung naked over the back of a horse, with a noose round his neck: the treatment that would have been given to a common criminal. He was taken to Leicester, where he was buried. The usurper had been usurped. He was the last King of England to die in battle.

The story has a curious coda. In September 2012, Richard's bones were discovered beneath a car park in Leicester, by local archaeologists responding to a campaign by the Richard III Society. They had together established, by an admirable piece of detective work, the site of his grave at Greyfriars, a Franciscan religious house demolished in 1538 following the dissolution of the monasteries.

The king's skeleton bore the traces of ten wounds, including two lethal blows to the base of the skull, and DNA tests confirmed that the bones were his. He did indeed suffer from curvature of the spine, but experts said he would not have looked hunch-backed, and the general tendency was to insist that he could have led a normal life. Thousands of people came to see his coffin in March 2015, in the days before he was reburied in Leicester Cathedral. More than half a millennium after his death, Richard had almost become popular.

HENRY VII

1485–1509

Although Henry VII won his crown on the battlefield, he ruled with the efficiency of an accountant rather than the panache of a warlord. He was born in Wales and imposed peace on England by establishing a strong new dynasty, the Tudors. When he died, he left to his son a united country, a submissive nobility and a vast amount of money.

His fugitive youth, and the disordered state of England, gave him good reason to strive for stability. He was born in 1457, soon after the outbreak of the Wars of the Roses, for most of which the Tudors found themselves on the losing side. His mother, Margaret Beaufort, was only thirteen when she gave birth to him in Pembroke Castle, and was already a widow, for her husband, Edmund Tudor, had perished in Carmarthen Castle after being captured by the Yorkists. Henry's grandfather, Owen Tudor, was executed by the Yorkists a few years later.

His parents gave him two rather tenuous links to the throne. The less significant was through Owen Tudor, a Welshman who had secretly married Catherine, the widow of Henry V. The more convincing was through Margaret Beaufort, a woman of formidable ability and enormous wealth who was descended from John of Gaunt, Duke of Lancaster, one of the sons of Edward III. But this connection had been declared illegitimate, the weak link being John of Gaunt's marriage to Catherine Swynford, which only took place after their children were born.

Henry's earliest years were spent in Wales, under the protection of his uncle, Jasper Tudor, but in 1471 the two of them fled to the court of the Duke of Brittany. For with the death of Henry VI, and of that king's only son, Edward, Henry had become the Lancastrian claimant to the throne: a position of mortal danger, should he ever fall into the hands of the Yorkists.

Edward IV tried and failed to get Henry back from Brittany. After the death in 1483 of that Yorkist king, and the disappearance of his two sons, presumed murdered, his younger brother seized the throne as Richard III. Here was Henry's chance to unify the opposition to the new and unpopular king. By promising, if he were crowned, to marry Elizabeth of York, daughter of Edward IV and Elizabeth Woodville, he became the candidate who could end the thirty-year struggle between the Lancastrians and the Yorkists.

But the first attempt to overthrow Richard III failed. The Duke of Buckingham mounted the coup too soon, and was slain before Henry could land in England. His supporters instead fled for their lives to join him in Brittany. Richard III attempted, by bribery, to have his rival extradited, but Henry escaped into French territory with an hour to spare.

In August 1485 came the second attempt. Henry landed in the far west of Wales, at Milford Haven, close to his birthplace of Pembroke. He had a small and unreliable force, lent to him by the King of France, but the Welsh bards welcomed him as one of their own, and substantial numbers of Welshmen volunteered to fight for him. As his standard he flew the red dragon of Cadwallader, who had been, in the seventh century, the last Welsh king to claim lordship over the whole of Britain.

Here was another element in the Tudors' assertion of legitimacy: they proclaimed themselves the descendants of the ancient British kings, which made them the lawful successors of no less a figure than King Arthur. A less flattering way of describing them would be as a family of obscure but boastful Welsh gentry. Richard III dismissed his adversary as 'an unknown Welshman'.

Henry deputed the command of his mixed force to the Earl of Oxford, an experienced soldier. After marching via Shrewsbury into the Midlands, they defeated and killed Richard III at Bosworth Field.

The new king knew little of the country he had gained: he had never lived there. But he well understood that to be King of England was a perilous undertaking. Of the nine monarchs who preceded Henry VII, four had been deposed and murdered, one had been killed in battle, and the other four died of illness.

Henry took the precaution of raising a bodyguard for himself: the first Yeomen of the Guard, who exist to this day at the Tower of London. Their duties included checking his food for poison and his mattress for hidden daggers. He got Parliament and the Pope to declare him and his descendants the lawful rulers of England. And he set about demonstrating that the war was over.

With his marriage early in 1486 to Elizabeth of York, a handsome woman, tall and fair with long golden hair, he reunited the houses of Lancaster and York. Their marriage had been arranged, in part by their mothers, as an act of policy, but they became very fond of each other. Their first son was born in September 1486, and named Arthur 'in honour of the British race', once ruled by the legendary King Arthur. For young Arthur and the newly united country, a glorious future was foreseen.

To symbolise this unity, the Tudor rose was devised, a botanically implausible combination of Lancastrian red and Yorkist white, and was reproduced everywhere.

But not everyone agreed that the Wars of the Roses were over. Henry had taken the precaution, after Bosworth, of imprisoning the ten-year-old Earl of Warwick, who had Plantagenet blood, so was expected to become the new Yorkist candidate for the throne. But in Ireland, a pretender landed with 2,000 German mercenaries, persuaded people that he was indeed the Earl of Warwick, and was crowned in Dublin as Edward VI. In 1487, these rebels landed in the north of England. They were defeated at the Battle of Stoke, and their candidate was unmasked as a boy called Lambert Simnel. Henry treated this dupe with clemency, and put him to work in the royal kitchens as a turnspit.

A second pretender appeared in 1492. Perkin Warbeck claimed to be the younger of the two princes in the Tower, and made a nuisance of himself for six years. Henry imprisoned him, but on learning of a plot by Warbeck to liberate Warwick, lost patience and had both of them executed.

Many members of the nobility had been killed during the Wars of the Roses. In order to curb the power of those overmighty subjects who remained, Henry imposed strict limits on the number of retainers they could keep. On one occasion the Earl of Oxford received the king at his castle. To do him honour, the earl lined up his liveried retainers along the approach. Chatting amiably, Henry carefully counted the retainers, and found they exceeded the legal number. He said, 'Thank you, My Lord, for the noble entertainment – and I shall see you within the week at my Court of Star Chamber.' The Star Chamber was a court through which much business was transacted, generally on terms favourable to the Crown. The earl received a crippling fine.

Here was a king who imposed himself on his subjects by excelling at business rather than at war. He liked to go through the accounts himself, and also employed tax collectors who would not take no for an answer. One of these, Cardinal Morton, gave his name to the expression 'Morton's fork', from the argument, impossible to evade, which he used to raise benevolences, or forced loans, for the king. For when Morton came on a supposedly rich man who was leading a frugal life, he said this meant large savings must exist, while if the man was throwing money around on luxuries, Morton said this meant he must be rich.

When Parliament clamoured for an expedition against the French, to revive the glories of the Hundred Years War, Henry reluctantly agreed, on condition that he was given a huge subsidy. He proceeded to raise a small force and land on the French coast, where he warned the French king that this was the prelude to a full-scale invasion. The king produced a large sum to buy him off, and Henry returned home and dismissed his little army. This was Henry's idea of a perfect war: no fighting, no blood and vast profit. He secured England's northern border by marrying his daughter, Margaret, to James IV of Scotland: an alliance that a century later would bring about the union of the two crowns.

For Henry's heir, Prince Arthur, a grand match was arranged

with Katherine of Aragon, daughter of Ferdinand and Isabella of Spain. They were married in 1501 at St Paul's Cathedral, but less than five months later, the prince, who was fifteen, died of consumption. This was a devastating blow to Henry and Elizabeth, and in 1502 the queen herself died a week after giving birth to their eighth child, a girl who did not survive. Henry himself became sick with grief, and would only allow his mother, Margaret Beaufort, near him. He appears never to have been happy again.

The historian Polydore Vergil left this description of Henry:

> His body was slender but well built and strong; his height above the average. His appearance was remarkably attractive and his face was cheerful, especially when speaking; his eyes were small and blue, his teeth few, poor and blackish; his hair was thin and white; his complexion sallow. His spirit was distinguished, wise and prudent; his mind was brave and resolute and never, even at moments of the greatest danger, deserted him . . . In government he was shrewd and prudent, so that no one dared to get the better of him through deceit or guile.

Vergil added, however, that 'all these virtues were obscured latterly only by avarice . . . This avarice is surely a bad enough vice in a private individual, whom it forever torments; in a monarch indeed it may be considered the worst vice, since it is harmful to everyone, and distorts those qualities of trustfulness, justice and integrity by which the state must be governed.'

Efficiency in collecting taxes is an uncharming characteristic, and Henry by the end of his reign was deeply unpopular. George Osborne, who became Chancellor of the Exchequer in 2010, has nevertheless named him as his favourite King of England.

HENRY VIII

1509–1547

No English monarch has treated those close to him with such ruthlessness as Henry VIII. The older he got, the more often he behaved like a petulant, self-obsessed teenager with a loaded revolver. His air of menace was magnified by the inability of those around him to read his mind. As Henry himself once said, 'If I thought that my cap knew what I was thinking, I would throw it in the fire.'

But by his determination to get his own way, Henry made England independent. He created the sovereign English nation, living under its own laws and guarded by its own ships.

The new king was from his boyhood a showman, with a genius for playing to the gallery. His tyranny was terrifying, but it was also popular: by taking the Pope's powers for himself, and seizing the Church's property, he expressed a widespread anti-clericalism, and made the growth of Protestantism serve his own purposes. He was an appallingly dangerous man to marry, or to work for, but as with the villain in a horror movie, that was part of his fascination. Holbein's portrait of him is unforgettable: here is a ruler it would be fatal to defy. Half a millennium later, he remains the most recognisable of all our kings, and in some ways the greatest.

And yet he was not expected to become king. He was the second son of Henry VII, and aged ten was conspicuous by the vigour of his dancing at the festivities to celebrate the marriage of Arthur, his older brother, to Katherine of Aragon. If Arthur had lived, and had heirs, Henry might be long forgotten. But within five months of the wedding feast, Arthur was dead.

At the age of seventeen, Henry VIII ascended the throne. Lord Mountjoy describes, in a letter, the rapture with which the young monarch was received: 'The heavens laugh, the earth exalts! Avarice is expelled from the country. Liberality scatters wealth with bounteous hand!' In place of a glum and miserly father came a brilliant young prince who spent extravagantly on every kind of festivity.

Henry was a magnificent figure of a man, and possessed a natural authority. One observer called him 'the handsomest ruler I ever set eyes on – a well-turned calf, tall, bright and fair of face, auburn hair, and round and beautiful face'. No supermodel could be prouder of her legs than Henry was of his. But he was also a devout theologian, skilful linguist, gifted musician, excellent tennis player, wonderful archer and jouster: in the eyes of his subjects, and of himself, a Renaissance prince.

One of the king's first acts was to marry Katherine of Aragon, who was now twenty-three. A papal dispensation had to be obtained for this match, since marriage to a brother's widow was not normally allowed by the Church.

Another early decision was to imprison two of his father's most faithful but hated servants, Empson and Dudley. They were tax gatherers who had enforced Henry VII's crushing financial demands. Henry VIII had them executed on trumped-up charges of treason. Already he was able to move with sudden mercilessness against those who were entitled to his protection.

Henry itched for the glories of war. For a few years, his father's counsellors held him back. But in 1512 he sent an army to Gascony: it returned bankrupt and diseased. The following year, he himself led an army to Calais, the one remaining English possession on the continent. It won some footling victories at huge financial cost. Meanwhile the Scots took the chance to invade England, but suffered a crushing defeat at the Battle of Flodden.

The logistics for the French campaign were organised by Thomas Wolsey, an obscure but emerging cleric. Perhaps because they were new, the Tudors preferred to employ new men: Wolsey's father was said to have been a butcher in Ipswich. Thomas's great abilities took him to Magdalen College, Oxford, and a meteoric rise within the Church, culminating in three great appointments: Archbishop of York in 1514, Lord Chancellor in 1515, Cardinal in 1518.

Wolsey spared his royal master the tedium of government. He would send Henry extracts from important documents: 'it should be painful for Your Grace to read the whole treaty'. Soon Wolsey was in charge of everything, and was building palaces at Whitehall and Hampton Court which rivalled in splendour those of the king.

In 1515, Henry's position as the most glamorous young monarch in Christendom, to which he attached huge importance, was endangered by the accession of Francis I of France: strong, devilishly attractive and a good general who soon conquered northern Italy. Francis himself had a serious rival in Charles V of Spain.

When Henry felt sorry for himself, he was at his most dangerous. How could Wolsey soothe his royal master's wounded ego? In 1518, he did so by arranging the Peace of London, which enabled Henry to consider himself the arbiter of Europe: a role which would appeal in centuries to come to many an English statesman who, too weak to dominate the continent, could at least hope to maintain a balance of power, so no conqueror could threaten the British Isles.

At that moment, a truce was useful to both Francis I and Charles V, who were vying to become Holy Roman Emperor. Charles won that contest, so Henry veered back to an alliance with Francis.

The scene was set for the climax of Wolsey's diplomacy, the Field of Cloth of Gold, a fortnight of competitive extravagance which was supposed to cement and dramatise Anglo-French friendship. In the summer of 1520, Henry and his wife, Queen Katherine, embarked for Calais with 5,000 followers, including the entire top layer of Tudor society. A tent city was erected at Guisnes: signs off the motorway soon after leaving Calais direct the modern traveller to the site of the Camp du Drap d'Or.

Here were jousting, feasting, fireworks, music and wrestling. Henry challenged Francis to a wrestling match, and got thrown: a detail mentioned only in the French reports. Wolsey appeared on a mule, to show how humble he was, but the beast was clad in velvet and gold.

The cost of the jamboree was enormous, the wind and dust appalling, the results negligible. Within a year, Henry had made an alliance with Charles V, and within three years he was once more engaged in a war with France in which he was getting nowhere. He had long since run out of his huge inheritance, and several parliamentary grants were also exhausted, so Wolsey resorted to the 'Amicable Grant', a forced loan which was most unlikely ever to be repaid.

After many years of marriage, Henry was tiring of Katherine of Aragon. She was meant to provide him with a male heir, but to their grief, their firstborn child, a boy, died after six weeks, after which Katherine suffered a succession of miscarriages and still-births. The only survivor was a girl, Princess Mary, born in 1516.

By the mid-1520s Katherine was too old to have more children. Henry, who possessed an unlimited ability to believe whatever suited him, convinced himself that he had never been legally married to her: by marrying his dead brother's wife he had broken God's law, which was why she was unable to present him with a son and heir.

And he was infatuated with a new, much younger and more fashionable woman, the seductive, dark-eyed Anne Boleyn. At the age of thirty-seven, he wrote letters to her in the style of a lovelorn youth, expressing his longing to kiss her 'pretty dukkys', or breasts. In order to marry her, and father a legitimate son, he needed the Pope to declare his marriage with Katherine invalid. In 1527, Wolsey was entrusted with the task of obtaining this dispensation.

The cardinal got nowhere. For the Pope had that year fallen into the hands of Katherine's nephew, Charles V, and Katherine was determined to remain married. She insisted her first marriage, to Arthur, had never been consummated, and that Henry knew she came to him as a virgin. When the evidence was examined, the counterclaim was made that the boy Arthur had boasted of going 'six miles into Spain'.

The cardinal failed to get what the king was determined to have, so the cardinal must go. And since Wolsey had made innumerable enemies by conducting himself with insufferable grandeur, this too would be a popular move. In November 1530 he was arrested in York on suspicion of treason. He died, brokenhearted, on his way south to face trial. His residences at Whitehall and Hampton Court were taken over by Henry.

Wolsey's man of business, Thomas Cromwell, who was the gifted son of a drunken Putney brewer, advised Henry that in order to make the break with Katherine, it had become necessary to break with the Pope. This was, on the face of it, an outrageous suggestion: as recently as 1521, the Pope had conferred on Henry the title Fidei Defensor, Defender of the Faith, as a reward for writing a defence of the Church against Martin Luther, who was inciting German Catholics to rebel against Rome.

In his counterblast to Luther, Henry insisted: 'All the faithful honour and acknowledge the sacred Roman See for their mother and supreme.' Sir Thomas More, who revised Henry's text, advised him to be less categorical on this point, but the king would not listen.

Yet now he defied the Pope. The royal egoist would make the world conform to his desires, and hired new servants to enable him to do so. One was Thomas Cranmer, a fellow of Jesus College, Cambridge, who looked with favour on the king's matrimonial plans and suggested writing to European universities to get their support. One mark of Henry's genius is his ability to detect genius in others. In 1532, he wished to have Cranmer appointed Archbishop of Canterbury. The Pope resisted, but gave in when Henry, supported by Parliament, threatened to cut off Rome's payments from the English Church.

In January 1533, Henry secretly married Anne. It was essential to declare independence from Rome, so the new union could be declared legal. Parliament therefore passed the Act in Restraint of Appeals, which declared: 'This realm of England is an empire.'

No dispute could now be referred to the Pope's higher jurisdiction, and Cranmer ruled that Henry's marriage to Katherine had from the start been null and void.

Anne was pregnant, and in June was given a magnificent coronation at Westminster Abbey, the last queen to receive this honour separately from her husband. But Henry no longer had public opinion on his side: Anne noticed that the people did not cheer her with any enthusiasm as she passed by. The people's sympathies were with Katherine, who had been sent away to the country.

In September, Anne gave birth to a daughter, Elizabeth. The king was disappointed, but still hoped for a son. The Pope excommunicated Henry, who retaliated by getting Parliament to declare him Supreme Head of the Church in England. The king was, as Macaulay put it, 'an orthodox Catholic, except that he chose to be his own Pope'. Sir Thomas More, who had served Henry with distinction, refused to swear the Oath of Supremacy to him, and was executed.

Thomas Cromwell now offered to make Henry the richest ruler in Christendom by confiscating the lands and treasures of the monasteries, who owned at least a quarter of the land in England. As a pretext for this enormous act of plunder, the greatest destruction of art and architecture in English history, evidence was gathered of monks living in every kind of sin.

Parliament joined with moralistic zeal in the dismemberment of the Church. In 1536 the lesser monasteries were dissolved. This and the king's scandalous treatment of his wives provoked the Pilgrimage of Grace, an uprising by Catholics in the north of England. The rebels disbanded in return for a promise that their grievances would be looked at by Parliament, and a free pardon, after which about 200 of them were executed by courts martial.

Katherine of Aragon died of cancer in 1536, still insisting she was married to Henry. In the same month he suffered a serious accident while jousting: he was knocked out for two hours, and his legs were left with splinters from a shattered lance which turned to ulcers. Some historians date a deterioration in his character from this time, and certainly the pain did not improve his temper. But the corrupting effect of unbounded power on a man of imperious will is sufficient explanation for his willingness to have those who displeased him put to death.

Anne Boleyn by now displeased him very much. She put it about that he displayed 'neither talent nor vigour' in bed: an intolerable insult to the king's vanity, especially if there was any truth in it. And she discovered him with his new love, Jane Seymour, made a hysterical scene, cut her hand while tearing a locket from Jane's neck, and soon afterwards gave birth to a dead boy. She told Henry her miscarriage was his fault for carrying on with 'that wench Jane Seymour'. He replied with heavy menace: 'You shall get no more boys by me . . . I will speak with you when you are well.'

Cromwell had long since set spies on Anne, and in May 1536 the queen was suddenly sent to the Tower, accused of treason, adultery and incest. It was claimed that over a period of three years, she had procured five men, including her own brother, to 'violate' her. All five denied the charges, except a musician, Mark Smeaton, who cracked under torture; but all were executed.

Anne was sentenced either to be burned as a witch, or else beheaded, according to the king's pleasure. On 19 May 1536 she was beheaded by an expert executioner fetched over from Calais. He used, as instructed by Henry, a sword, and killed her with a single blow.

Archbishop Cranmer established that the king's marriage with Anne had all along been null and void, for Henry had slept some years before with her elder sister, and she herself had been promised to someone else. As soon as Anne was dead, Henry married the complaisant Jane Seymour, who in October 1537 gave birth to a son, Edward. The king wept with joy and across England bonfires were lit in celebration. But a fortnight later, Jane died of puerperal fever. Henry had her buried in the royal vault at Windsor, where one day he would lie beside a queen of whom he had not had time to tire.

Henry by now was very fat, and had ulcerated legs. In 1538, when one of these ulcers became clogged, a blood clot blocked his lung, and he became black in the face and speechless. Nor was the international situation reassuring: the Pope had excommunicated him, and was planning to send a grand coalition of the continental powers, plus Scotland, to overthrow him.

The king had for his whole reign spent heavily on warships, which were the primary way to defend England. He can fairly be regarded as the founder of the Royal Navy. He also spent lavishly on coastal fortifications.

And he looked about for a new wife. He wished to judge a beauty parade of all the eligible young women of Europe, to be held at Calais. Francis I of France observed that this would be more like a cattle market than a pageant from the days of King Arthur; and Henry was seen, for the only recorded time, to blush.

Cromwell proposed Anne of Cleves as a bride, for she would bring Henry a continental ally. Rashly the minister assured the king that Anne, a pockmarked thirty-four-year-old, was beautiful. Henry agreed to the match, but was horrified when he met 'the Flanders Mare', as he called her. In January 1540 he went through with the marriage, but was unable to consummate it, though he assured his physician, Dr Buttes, that he thought himself 'able to do the Act with other than with her'.

And soon there was just such a woman: the voluptuous Catherine Howard, nineteen-year-old niece of the Duke of Norfolk. The Howard family, who were enemies of the low-born Cromwell, told Henry that Catherine was in 'pure and honest condition'. Stephen Gardiner, Bishop of Winchester, arranged assignations for Henry with the sexy young woman at his house on the south bank of the Thames. The king was infatuated, and as soon as his marriage with Anne was annulled, he married Catherine.

In June that year, Henry had Cromwell arrested during a meeting of the Privy Council on a charge of high treason. In royal service, Cromwell had proved himself a great administrator, but no one now would defend him. In vain he wrote to the king: 'I call for mercy, mercy, mercy.' The House of Lords passed a Bill of Attainder in which he was condemned as a heretic and traitor, and he was executed at Tower Hill, after which his head was displayed on a spike on London Bridge.

The Catholic nobility, led by the Duke of Norfolk, rejoiced to see the end of this 'foul churl', who had promoted the Protestant faith. For England was in an indeterminate religious state, neither Roman Catholic nor Protestant, with a king who had shocked Christendom by destroying the shrine of Thomas à Becket at Canterbury, and the monasteries, but still considered himself a Catholic. The Bible was, however, issued in English, and Cranmer began the creation of his sublime English liturgy.

The forty-nine-year-old Henry showered Catherine, his intoxicating young wife, with jewels and lands, including Cromwell's estates. The king imagined himself once more young: there were feasts, jousts, pageants and masques. But in March 1541, his leg ulcer closed up again, and Henry was thrown into agony.

Catherine soon tired of being chained to an obese, immobile and evil-smelling invalid. She flirted with Thomas Culpeper, a handsome young courtier, and appointed a previous lover, Francis Dereham, as her private secretary. Henry at first laughed off reports of her infidelity, and insisted that God had given him a 'jewel of womanhood, and perfect love'. But then the whole story came out. Dereham confessed 'he had known her carnally many times both in his doublet and hose, between the sheets, and in naked bed'.

Henry gave way to murderous self-pity. He blubbered at a meeting of the Council, 'regretting his ill luck in meeting such ill-conditioned wives'. In February 1542, Catherine was taken by barge to the Tower – passing under the heads of her lovers, displayed on spikes on London Bridge – and was executed.

The king plunged into wars against Scotland and France. In 1539 he was, thanks to the dissolution of the monasteries, the richest monarch in Europe. By 1545 he had run out of money. He debased the coinage, initiated massive inflation and sold at knock-down prices vast tracts of monastic land which could have formed a permanent endowment for the Crown. But he made magnificent benefactions too: Trinity College, Cambridge, was formed as an amalgam of two earlier, smaller colleges, while Christ Church, Oxford, rose from the remnants of Cardinal College, founded by Wolsey.

In July 1543, he married his last wife, Catherine Parr: an amiable, well-educated widow from the Lake District. She soothed the bitter, self-absorbed tyrant, who was wracked by ulcers and fevers, and only able to move by means of litters or portable chairs.

Catherine also got on with and took an interest in the education of his three children: Mary by Katherine of Aragon, Elizabeth by Anne Boleyn, and Edward by Jane Seymour. But Henry never lost his murderous paranoia: in January 1547, he had the boastful young Earl of Surrey executed, and put Surrey's father, the Duke of Norfolk, in the Tower.

Henry had by now entered his last illness. No doctor dared tell him he was dying: to prophesy the death of the monarch was treason. But after dominating his country for almost thirty-eight years, he died in the Palace of Whitehall on 28 January 1547, with Cranmer at his side.

EDWARD VI

1547–1553

How fragile Edward VI looks, and how fragile he was. In the gorgeous portrait of him in the National Portrait Gallery, the young king tries to swagger like his father, Henry VIII, but is vulnerable rather than dominant. Edward was born at Hampton Court in October 1537. His mother, Jane Seymour, died of fever a fortnight later, and the longed-for son and heir was soon sent for the sake of his health to live in the country, looked after by nurses.

When he was four, he fell gravely ill with malaria. Once he was better, his stepmother, Catherine Parr, arranged for his education to be put in the hands of some of the best scholars of the day. Before he could read or write, he began to learn, by word of mouth, Latin and Greek as well as English. And he developed a sincere belief in Protestant doctrines.

He was only nine when his father died. Henry had made elaborate arrangements for a Council of Regency, to govern during his son's minority. But Henry dead no longer inspired fear, and Edward's maternal uncle, Edward Seymour, at once overthrew the Council and had himself established as Protector of the realm and sole guardian of the king, who created him Duke of Somerset.

Henry's religious settlement, which included the retention of Catholic doctrines, was likewise overthrown. England became, with the boy king's wholehearted approval, a Protestant country. Thomas Cranmer, Archbishop of Canterbury, had told him at his coronation that he was 'Supreme Head of the Church, elected of God, and only commanded by Him', and that his duty was to see 'God truly worshipped and idolatry destroyed'.

In 1549, the Book of Common Prayer was issued in English: a masterpiece which owed most to Cranmer. Its use was enforced by an Act of Uniformity. In 1552, a second and more radical prayer book was issued. The service of Holy Communion became no more than a commemorative rite, images were smashed in churches, and chantries, where prayers were offered for the souls of the dead, were closed. Some of the proceeds were used to found schools, named after Edward VI, which endure to this day in Birmingham and many other towns.

These measures, and severe economic distress, caused uprisings in 1549 in the West Country and in East Anglia, where the rebels were routed by John Dudley, son of Henry VII's executed tax gatherer. Dudley proceeded to outmanoeuvre Protector

Somerset, whom he consigned to the Tower and had executed. Edward wrote in his diary: 'Today, the Duke of Somerset had his head cut off on Tower Hill.'

Dudley became Duke of Northumberland. His power rested on his control of the king, who was plainly not long for this world: and when Edward died, he would be succeeded by his older sister, Mary, who was a devout Roman Catholic. To avert this disaster, Northumberland hatched a desperate and self-serving plot. He married his son to Lady Jane Grey, a great-granddaughter of Henry VII, and got Edward to 'devise' the throne to this devout Protestant.

Lady Jane, who was fifteen, was reluctant to go through with the scheme. But after Edward's death from tuberculosis on 6 July 1553, Northumberland had her proclaimed queen and she entered the Tower of London amid great pomp, wearing platform soles in order to make her appear taller.

Neither the nobility nor the people were prepared to accept this coup. Lady Jane's reign lasted nine days. Northumberland's soldiers deserted him. He was arrested and executed. The penalty of political failure was still death. Lady Jane and her husband were convicted of treason and confined to the Tower, but were not executed until February 1554, by which time they had become quite fond of each other.

MARY I

1553–1558

Mary was the first queen to rule over England, and also the saddest. Like her father, Henry VIII, she insisted on getting her own way, but unlike him she had no gift for carrying the people with her. Mary was a devout Roman Catholic who believed it was her duty to return her subjects to that religion, and tried to do so by burning at least 287 of them at the stake, or one every five days during the period of her persecution.

Few campaigns have been more counterproductive. The queen instead fostered England's idea of itself as a Protestant nation, whose faithful members suffered martyrdom in flames lit on the orders of 'Bloody Mary', as she later became known.

She was the one surviving child of Henry's first wife, Katherine of Aragon, and long before ascending, at the age of thirty-seven, the throne, had suffered bitter humiliations. Henry was addicted, as part of his diplomacy, to arranging to marry her into other royal houses, and when she was only two he got her betrothed to the dauphin, the son of the King of France. A French dignitary came over to take part in the ceremony, and the perky princess asked him: 'Are you the dauphin? If you are, I want to kiss you.'

As she got older, she became less perky. She was a pretty young woman, with bright eyes and reddish hair, but her father never presented her with a husband to kiss. As Mary recognised once she was grown up, 'while my father lives I shall only be the Lady Mary, the most unhappy lady in Christendom'. She suffered from depression, menstrual troubles and poor eyesight. And by this point, she had undergone the agony of her father turning against her much-loved mother.

Henry convinced himself he had never been married to Katherine of Aragon: a claim which had the effect of making their daughter illegitimate. Mary sided with her mother, who protested that the marriage had all along been valid, and pointed out that neither Henry's father nor her own would have accepted anything less. Katherine was overruled, sent away into the country, and a few years later died.

Mary now had a stepmother, Anne Boleyn, who referred to her as 'the cursed bastard'. Anne soon gave birth to a daughter, Elizabeth, on whom the seventeen-year-old Mary was made to wait. The rift between her and her father was deepened by Mary's refusal to recognise him as Supreme Head of the Church. She was clever and well educated, but possessed a streak of embittered obstinacy which made it difficult for her to know when to make concessions. And on the question of her Roman Catholic faith, she regarded it as a matter of conscience not to give in.

Thomas Cromwell with great difficulty managed to persuade Mary to submit outwardly to Henry on the question of royal supremacy over the Church, though inwardly she remained a staunch supporter of papal supremacy. Father and daughter could now be reconciled: a process fostered by Henry's last wife, Catherine Parr. In 1544, it was settled that Henry's three children, Edward, Mary and Elizabeth, would succeed him in that order, though any children of Edward would of course take precedence over his sisters.

Throughout her brother's reign, Mary continued, despite his reproaches, to hear the Roman Catholic Mass. When Edward realised he was dying, he tried to deny her the throne by arranging for Lady Jane Grey, who was Protestant, to become queen. But this brazen subversion of Henry VIII's wishes was unpopular, and the Duke of Northumberland, who led the coup, failed to lure Mary into his hands.

She instead withdrew for a few days to Suffolk, where she had strong support, and waited for the rebellion to collapse, which it did without a fight. Mary entered London in triumph. She was at this moment a popular monarch. As often happens at the start of a reign, people wanted to believe in her.

Mary repelled their enthusiasm with alarming swiftness. In order to bring about a permanent return to Roman Catholicism, she needed to produce an heir: otherwise she would be succeeded by her younger sister, Elizabeth, who had Protestant tendencies.

The new queen was thirty-seven years old, and her health had never been good, so there was no time to lose. She did not wish to marry one of her subjects, so sought advice from Simon Renard, ambassador of the emperor Charles V, about eligible men. To him she confessed that she had 'never felt that which is called love, nor harboured thoughts of voluptuousness'. In other words, she had no idea what she was doing, but imagined her severe ideas of religion were a guide in worldly questions too. She decided to marry Philip of Spain, the son of Renard's employer.

She could not have made a more disastrous choice. Philip was un-English, and uninterested in England. He was a fervent Catholic who intended to use England for Spanish purposes. The English recognised him as a mortal threat to national independence, and the Commons begged her to think again, something Mary was seldom inclined to do.

In January 1554, Sir Thomas Wyatt led a rising in Kent which was meant to be part of a wider rebellion that would force her to reconsider the match. But Wyatt was defeated, and Mary felt impelled to take a harder line against opponents. She concluded that her immediate predecessor, her cousin Lady Jane Grey, must be executed.

Mary and Philip were married in the summer of 1554, and his head appeared on English coins. But it was soon clear that private happiness would do nothing to compensate for political difficulties. Philip was eleven years younger than her and found her physically repulsive. Just over a year later, he returned to Spain.

Mary not only insisted she loved him: like the Virgin Mary, she announced to the world that a 'babe had stirred in her womb'. The Venetian ambassador described her when she ascended the throne as 'always pale and emaciated', but now she began to put on weight. Amid great rejoicings, preparations were made for her child's birth. But in her desperation for a child, Mary had deceived herself, and made herself ridiculous: this was a phantom, or hysterical, pregnancy.

In November 1554, Parliament repealed Henry VIII's Act of

Supremacy and restored papal authority. It also re-enacted the Heresy Act of 1401, which allowed burning at the stake, but had been abolished under Edward VI: in his reign, Dissenters were usually imprisoned rather than burned.

In February 1555, the burning of Protestant heretics began, and continued until Mary's death in November 1558. Her predecessors had done this too: Henry VII burned ten heretics in twenty-four years, Henry VIII eighty-one in thirty-eight years, and two perished in this way in the reign of Edward VI. So for Mary to burn 287 in little more than three years was a conspicuous increase in the rate of persecution.

The burnings, which took place all over southern England, were reminiscent of the Spanish Inquisition at its worst. They promoted the fear that Mary was imposing an alien tyranny, and they did not render England obedient. Onlookers often sympathised with the unfortunate victim. The English were growing ever more insular and xenophobic, and Roman Catholicism came to be seen as foreign, a prejudice that would endure into the early twentieth century.

The burnings offered the chance to Mary's Protestant opponents to show they were dying for a cause in which they truly believed. The Church of England derived a great part of its validity from the bravery shown by its martyrs under this queen. For several centuries, the words spoken by Hugh Latimer to his fellow bishop, Nicholas Ridley, before they were burned at the stake in Oxford, were known to everyone brought up in the Anglican tradition: 'Be of good comfort, Master Ridley, and play the man. We shall this day light such a candle by God's grace in England, as (I trust) shall never be put out.'

Still more famous was the story of Cranmer, Archbishop of Canterbury, who had done more than any other churchman to make England a Protestant country. Cranmer was arrested, and at first he recanted. But then, to the dismay of Mary's supporters, he in public recanted his recantation, and said the hand with which he had signed it would be the first to be burned. So as the flames rose about him in Oxford, he held his right hand to the fire. This timid scholar had conquered his fears and created a national Church. John Foxe ensured, by writing his *Book of Martyrs*, that every refinement of Marian cruelty would be known to the English for centuries to come. His masterpiece of Protestant propaganda, fully illustrated with woodcuts, was first published in 1563, and was placed in every English parish church.

To set against these horrors, which only she could have halted, Mary had no successes. In January 1558, Calais, the last English possession on the continent of Europe, fell to the French. Mary felt this humiliation deeply: she said that when she died, and was opened, 'Calais' would be found graven upon her heart. Once again she fancied herself pregnant, and once again she was wrong. In November 1558 the barren queen died, probably of uterine cancer, at St James's Palace.

ELIZABETH I

1558–1603

Elizabeth I's reign developed into a love affair with her people, and with every eligible man, conducted in many different moods: teasing, flirtatious, romantic, haughty, procrastinating. In 1588 it reached its ecstatic climax when together they defied the Armada sent by Philip of Spain to subdue them.

She was the last of the Tudors. In newly rich families, the founder accumulates the fortune and lives in a restrained way; the heir is ostentatious and incapable of self-control; and the third generation often proves so feeble it loses control of the business. The Tudors looked more and more likely to conform to this pattern. Henry VII established the dynasty, his son Henry VIII governed with magnificent self-indulgence, and in the third generation it seemed that the family had gone into precipitate decline, with Edward VI too young, and his older sister Mary too bigoted, to impose royal authority.

Another sister remained: Elizabeth, Henry VIII's daughter by Anne Boleyn. But Mary had shown how hard it was to be a woman in power. The Venetian ambassador expressed the view that 'statecraft is no business for ladies': though that remark was prompted by Mary, Queen of Scots, to whose downfall we shall come.

Elizabeth was sitting under an oak tree at Hatfield, in Hertfordshire, when she heard her half-sister had died. She was twenty-five years old, and had already endured much: her mother's execution, the stigma of bastardy, sexual harassment when she was fourteen by Thomas Seymour (a handsome but imprudent man, soon afterwards executed for plotting against his older brother, Protector Somerset), imprisonment in the Tower of London followed by house arrest in the country, cross-examination for evidence of treason which, had it been discovered, would have led to her death.

As one of her first actions, the new queen made Sir William Cecil her principal secretary. He served her with unfailing industry and perspicacity for the next forty years. The term 'meritocracy' would not be coined until the reign of Elizabeth II, but Elizabeth I was the outstanding meritocrat of her age. She employed highly able ministers, but was herself as able as any of them, and never became their prisoner. Throughout her reign, Elizabeth made the decisions, which were often not those her advisers were pleading with her to make. She conversed with perfect ease in Latin, French and Italian, and was as skilled as any professional diplomat in the art of concealing her own hand, while discovering the cards, often stronger than her own, held by her opponents. She was extraordinarily good at seeing what everyone else was trying to do, while veiling her intentions.

But she was no mere manipulator. The Spanish ambassador, Count de Feria, was unwise enough to tell her she owed her throne to his master, Philip of Spain, the widower of her sister, Mary. She put him right, and told him it was actually the people who had placed her on the throne. As Feria wrote after this encounter: 'She is much attached to the people, and is very confident that they are all on her side; which is indeed true.'

How carefully she put off that confrontation for as long as it could be put off. Spain was far richer and stronger than England, and was the champion of English Catholicism, which could still draw on deep reserves of loyalty: the death in the last years of Elizabeth's reign of hundreds of Catholic martyrs would show that. English Protestants already had their hundreds of martyrs, created in the last years by Mary. The conditions existed for religious civil war, as seen in France.

The new queen averted this danger by pursuing a *via media*, or middle way, between the two sides. The Church of England was both Catholic and Protestant. This displeased purists, but pragmatists could see its advantages. Elizabeth demanded no more than an outward conformity.

Toleration was not at this time acceptable: people regarded it with horror, and believed that for a country to be secure, it must have only one religion. The queen nevertheless practised, in her subtle way, a degree of toleration, avoiding the extremes to which Edward VI and Mary had been so inflexibly attached. When the question arose of whether she expected people to make the sign of the cross as they used to in the old Catholic days, Elizabeth took the view, 'All can, none must, some ought.' T. S. Eliot, one of the great poets of the twentieth century, wrote of this time: 'In its persistence in finding a mean between Papacy and Presbytery the English Church under Elizabeth became something representative of the finest spirit of England.'

There was a risk this work would never take root, and would be overthrown by Elizabeth's early death, either from disease or at the hands of an assassin. The universal assumption was that she would get married, in order to produce an heir. Otherwise the throne might pass, on her death, to her cousin, Mary, Queen of Scots, who was a Roman Catholic, brought up in France and married to the heir to the French throne.

The English liked the idea of being dominated by France no better than they had liked, in the previous reign, the idea of being dominated by Spain. The Commons implored Elizabeth to marry. She replied that she would not mind if she 'lived and died a virgin'. This was not taken seriously. Every eligible bachelor in Europe tried to win her hand, and so did some of her most dashing courtiers.

Like many of the great flirts, she was not a classical beauty. But she had beautiful eyes and hands, and was so witty, so animated, so ready to take amusement in advancing and withdrawing. The queen was powerful, but she was also a woman. She had a gift for amorous friendship, and liked it very much when people were in love with her. Her admirers included the Earl of Leicester, known to her as 'sweet Robin'.

But still she did not marry. Her sister's marriage had been a disaster, and her father's six marriages were not encouraging. If Elizabeth got her choice of husband wrong, she could lose everything.

Mary, Queen of Scots, young, beautiful, well educated and often madly incautious, was less reticent about getting it wrong. Her first husband died soon after ascending the French throne, whereupon she returned to Scotland and was crowned queen of that country, which was bitterly divided between Roman Catholics and increasingly extreme Protestants. At the age of twenty-three she married her cousin, Lord Darnley, who like her was descended from Henry VII, and conceived a son, the future James VI of Scotland and James I of England.

But she and her husband very soon fell out, and even before James was born, Darnley joined a conspiracy of Protestant lords to murder David Riccio, an Italian musician to whom Mary had become insultingly close. They came on Riccio as he was at supper with the queen at Holyrood Palace. He clung in terror to her dress and pleaded for her to save him, but Darnley and six others dragged him from the room and killed him with at least fifty-three dagger wounds. So violent was his death, one is surprised Quentin Tarantino has not yet filmed it.

Mary was six months pregnant, but remarked in a calm tone: 'I will think upon a revenge.' She lured Darnley to a house on the edge of Edinburgh, which one night was destroyed in a huge explosion soon after she had left him: his body was found in the garden. The main perpetrator of this atrocity was the Earl of Bothwell, a dissolute brigand who now carried Mary off, with her consent, and became her third husband.

This imprudent marriage united the fractious Scottish nobility against their queen, and in 1567 she was forced to abdicate in favour of her infant son, and flee for her life to England, where she was confined to a succession of castles and country houses.

There were now two queens in England: and Mary believed, as did many English Catholics, that she had every right to try to overthrow Elizabeth, who in their eyes was 'an incestuous bastard, begotten and born in sin of an infamous courtesan, Anne Boleyn'. In 1569, a Catholic rising in the north of England was put down with severe reprisals: about 600 of the rebels were hanged. In 1570, the Pope excommunicated Elizabeth.

Mary engaged, with characteristic recklessness, in plot after plot against Elizabeth. Her secret communications were regularly intercepted: sometimes they were sent by channels which had actually been set up by the Elizabethan secret service, organised by Francis Walsingham. It was known exactly what she was trying to do: yet for twenty years, Elizabeth resisted entreaties to have her put to death. For an anointed queen to consent to the judicial execution of her own kinswoman, another anointed queen, was a terrible thing. By the standards of that time, to murder her would have been far less bad.

But in 1586, the Babington Plot was exposed: a particularly flagrant attempt to murder Elizabeth, rescue Mary and invade England with a foreign force. The country was in uproar, swept by rumours of invasion by one or other of the two great Catholic powers, Spain and France. Babington and his fellow conspirators were put to death, and Parliament petitioned for the immediate execution of Mary. Elizabeth would not at first yield, and sent Parliament 'an answer-answerless'. But in February 1587, she signed the death warrant.

In life, Mary had often been foolish. Facing death in Fotheringhay Castle, Northamptonshire, she was magnificent. To the end, she denied her guilt, and resisted exhortations to abandon her Roman Catholic faith. She was perfectly composed as she laid her head on the block and said in a loud voice, 'In manus tuas, Domine, confide spiritum meum' – 'Into thy hands, O Lord, I commend my spirit'.

When the executioner held up her head, declaring 'God save the queen', it fell to the ground, and he was left holding what turned out to be a wig. Her own close-cropped hair had turned grey during her captivity. Her dog, a Skye terrier, emerged from beneath her petticoat, where it had hidden itself, and placed itself between its mistress's head and her shoulders.

Elizabeth was grief-stricken at the news of Mary's death, but her people rejoiced: bells were rung, guns fired, bonfires lit. The threat of Catholic invasion was at its height, for Philip of Spain was known to be amassing a great armada which he intended to send against England. He had ten times the resources of Elizabeth, who needed to be, and was, as parsimonious as her grandfather, Henry VII. She could not afford to pay for a fleet which would match Philip's in size. England's maritime development was instead driven forward by adventurers excited by the vast profits to be made by plundering Spanish treasure ships on their way home from South America. The most famous of these privateers was Sir Francis Drake, who in 1577–80 made his great circum-navigation of the globe, during which he plundered the Pacific coast of Latin America and made a profit of 4,700 per cent for his backers (including Elizabeth).

Philip regarded this as piracy, but to the English it was a glori-ously patriotic venture, fully justified by the threat from Catholic Spain. Drake urged attack as the best form of defence. In April 1587, he sailed into Cadiz, where in his words he singed the King of Spain's beard, destroying vast quantities of shipping and stores. The English ships had better long-range guns, which rendered the enemy's galleys powerless. The national weapon was no longer the longbow, which brought victories on land, but the broadside fired from a highly manoeuvrable and expertly navigated ship, which would see Englishmen conquer the oceans of the world.

On 19 July 1588 the Spanish Armada was sighted off Cornwall. The English, under the command of Lord Howard of Effingham, with Drake as his deputy, with difficulty got out of Plymouth: the winds were against them. On 21 July, the two fleets met, and began a running battle up the Channel. The Spanish plan was to join with the Duke of Parma in the Netherlands and bring his formidable army across the Channel. On 27 July, they anchored off Calais. The English attacked them with fireships, forced them to cut their anchor ropes, engaged them in battle off Gravelines, almost drove them on to the Zealand banks before the Dutch coast, and then, with a change of wind, pursued them into the North Sea.

In England, the danger of an invasion by Parma still appeared acute. Elizabeth went down to her army at Tilbury and delivered the most celebrated speech by any English monarch:

> My loving people, we have been persuaded by some that are careful of our safety, to take heed how we commit ourselves to armed multitudes, for fear of treachery. But I assure you, I do not desire to live to distrust my faithful and loving people. Let tyrants fear. I have always so behaved myself that, under God, I have placed my chiefest strength and safeguard in the loyal hearts and goodwill of my subjects; and therefore I am come amongst you, as you see, at this time, not for my recreation and disport, but being resolved, in the midst and heat of the battle, to live or die amongst you all, to lay down for my God, and for my kingdom, and for my people, my honour and my blood, even in the dust. I know I have the body of a weak and feeble woman, but I have the heart and stomach of a king, and of a king of England too, and think foul scorn that Parma or Spain, or any prince of Europe should dare to invade the borders of my realm.

It was characteristic of Elizabeth to turn her weakness into a way of proclaiming courage, confidence and unity. She went on, with her usual grasp of practicalities, to assure her troops that they would be 'duly paid'. Soldiers at this time very often did not get paid. Her economies enabled her to honour her debts.

The Armada, driven far past the waiting Parma, was harried by the English as far north as Edinburgh. The Spanish saw that their only hope, though running short of food and water and without the anchors left off Calais, was to flee home round Scotland and Ireland. On those coasts great numbers of ships were wrecked, so they lost a third of their fleet.

Protestants everywhere rejoiced at England's victory, and even the Pope expressed his admiration of Elizabeth. Armada portraits show her as a majestic and glittering figure, her dress decorated with innumerable jewels, her hand resting on a globe. The Virgin Queen took care she should be shown as a goddess, but one capable of earthy human touches, as in this story about the Earl of Oxford, related by the antiquarian John Aubrey: 'This Earle of Oxford, making of his low obeisance to Queen Elizabeth, happened to let a Fart, at which he was so abashed and ashamed that he went to Travell, 7 yeares. On his returne the Queen welcomed him home, and sayd, My Lord, I had forgott the Fart.'

Although Catholicism had emerged so clearly as the enemy, the queen did not approve of extreme Protestantism. Catholic priests, who with unwavering courage came to England to uphold their faith, were put to death when discovered, but Puritans were not permitted to take over the Church of England. At Elizabeth's command, the bishops crushed incipient Presbyterianism.

She had one last favourite, the glamorous and reckless Earl of Essex, but he overplayed his hand, imagined he could dominate the queen, and was himself put to death in 1601. In the same year, she delivered her Golden Speech, in which she told Parliament: 'And though you have had, and may have, many princes more mighty and wise, sitting in this state, yet you never had, or shall have, any that will be more careful and loving.'

To the end, Elizabeth never named her successor. She knew how dangerous it was to have one, and that careful arrangements were actually being made by Robert Cecil for James VI of Scotland to take over when the time came. In March 1603, she was plainly dying. Cecil told her she must go to bed, to which she retorted: 'Little man, little man, "must" is not a word to use to princes.' For three days she sat fully dressed in her palace at Richmond, without speaking, on a heap of cushions in her audience chamber, and then she died.

JAMES I
1603–1625

The first member of the Stuart dynasty presented a startling contrast to his predecessor. In place of their magnificent and dignified queen, the English found themselves with a shambling, slobbering, dishevelled king who spoke in a barely comprehensible Scottish accent. His tongue was too big for his mouth and this arthritic, gout-ridden thirty-six-year-old was in the habit of falling in love with beautiful young men, while taking no trouble to win the approval of anyone else.

There was nevertheless general relief that the succession had occurred without a drop of blood being spilt. James himself was in no doubt of his high royal status. He had never known any other life, and was descended through both his parents from Margaret Tudor, daughter of Henry VII.

In 1567, at the age of thirteen months, Charles James Stuart, to give him his full name, was crowned James VI, King of Scots. His mother, Mary, Queen of Scots, was suspected of complicity in the murder of his father, Henry Stuart, Lord Darnley, and had made herself impossibly unpopular by marrying the ringleader of that crime, the Earl of Bothwell. She was forced to abdicate, and fled in danger of her life to England, where twenty years later she was executed for plotting against her cousin, Elizabeth I.

James in his boyhood was a pawn in the hands of the violently quarrelsome Scottish nobility and the Calvinistic Scottish Church, or Kirk. On two occasions he was kidnapped, and he acquired a lifelong fear of assassination which prompted him to wear thickly padded clothes. He also acquired an excellent classical education at the hands of a teacher, George Buchanan, who did not hesitate to beat him.

At the age of seventeen, James managed to manoeuvre himself into power, but made no more than token efforts to intercede on his mother's behalf. He married Anne of Denmark, by whom he had three children who survived infancy: Henry, Charles and Elizabeth. He was described by one observer as 'an old young man', for he took things with pedantic seriousness, and published works defending the doctrine of the divine right of kings: 'Kings are called Gods; they are appointed by God and answerable only to God.' His own life was transformed by becoming King of England.

On the way south, James was astonished that despite their luxuriousness, the country houses in which he stayed were not fortified against attack. England was far richer than Scotland, and far more peaceful. At Stamford Hill, just north of London, he was greeted by the Lord Mayor and aldermen, wearing velvet robes and gold chains, and by 500 'richly apparelled' citizens, including nine actors, among them William Shakespeare.

An early sign of the king's trust in his own judgement came in his *Counterblast to Tobacco*, in which he condemned the then new pastime of smoking: 'A custom loathsome to the eye, hateful to the nose, harmful to the brain, dangerous to the lungs, and in the black, stinking fume thereof, nearest resembling the horrible Stygian smoke of the pit that is bottomless.'

James aspired to unify his two kingdoms, England and Scotland, and invented the name Great Britain for them. As he told Parliament: 'Hath not God first united these Two Kingdoms both in Language, Religion and Similitude of Manners? Yea, hath he not made us all in One Island, compassed with One Sea?'

But the English had not the faintest desire to be united with the Scots. Nor was the religious question as settled as James implied. English Catholics hoped that because the new king's mother had been Catholic, he would treat them with indulgence. English Puritans hoped that because of his Scottish Presbyterian upbringing, the king would purify the Church of England by getting rid of bishops, sacraments, vestments and other rituals surviving from Catholic times.

James believed that as Supreme Head of the Church of England, and an expert theologian in his own right, it was for him to decide the way ahead. So he convened a conference at Hampton Court and ordered the preparation of a new translation of the Bible: the Authorised Version, which appeared in 1611 and rested on William Tyndale's translation made in the reign of Henry VIII. The King James Bible, as it is often known, is the most influential prose work in the English language, and also the most sublime, and the man who ordered its creation deserves some share of the credit for it.

He had the wit to continue Elizabeth's middle path in religion. At Hampton Court he disappointed devotees on both sides. 'No bishop, no king,' he told the Puritans, some of whom realised that to enjoy religious liberty, they would have to emigrate: in 1620 the Pilgrim Fathers set sail in the *Mayflower* for America.

Nor were the Catholics satisfied by the limited toleration extended towards them. The fiercer of them plotted the greatest act of terrorism ever devised on English soil. When Parliament met on 5 November 1605, they intended to destroy king, Lords and Commons in one mighty explosion.

One of the conspirators wrote anonymously to his brother-in-law, Lord Monteagle, warning him to stay away that day, for 'they shall receive a terrible blow . . . and yet they shall not see who hurts them'. Monteagle showed this mysterious letter to the Privy Council, who showed it to James. The king guessed it meant an explosion. It is likely that the astute Robert Cecil, whom he had retained as his chief minister, already knew through his network of spies what was afoot.

At midnight on 4 November, the cellars under the House of Lords were searched, and Guy Fawkes was caught with thirty-six barrels of gunpowder, along with a tinderbox. The defeat of the plot is celebrated to this day with bonfires on which a guy is burned. Guy Fawkes and his fellow conspirators were hanged, drawn and quartered.

James did not, however, conclude from this that it might be worth having Parliament on his side. The Stuarts saw Parliament as a troublesome institution, which if possible should be circumvented. As James told the Spanish ambassador in 1614: 'I am surprised that my ancestors should ever have permitted such an institution to come into existence. I am a stranger, and found it here when I arrived . . . I am obliged to put up with what I cannot get rid of.'

There is a saving touch of realism in the king's complaint: he knew he must put up with Parliament. But where Elizabeth would have charmed and conciliated MPs in order to get her own way, James hectored and antagonised them. With an intellectual's tendency to set a ridiculously high value on his own ideas, the king preached divine right at them. He had no sympathy with lawyer Members of Parliament such as Sir Edward Coke who developed the doctrine that they were upholding ancient privileges enshrined four centuries earlier in Magna Carta: a belief which enabled the king's opponents to demand more power for Parliament while regarding themselves as conservatives.

After Cecil's death in 1612, James relied on a series of favourites, of whom the most notorious was George Villiers, a remarkably beautiful young sycophant who was created Duke of Buckingham. James's pet name for him was 'Steenie', a reference to Stephen the martyr, who is said in the Acts of the Apostles to have had 'the face of an angel'.

The court, which was stuffed with Scottish hangers-on, disgusted the high-minded English Puritans: one of them lamented that the 'court caterpillars' consisted of 'fools and bawds, mimics and catamites'. The king was astonishingly extravagant, and this meant he had to ask Parliament for money. But MPs demanded redress of grievances before they would oblige him. In 1621, when they entered a protestation in their journal, James tore it out, and had several of them arrested.

James regarded foreign policy as one of his prerogatives, and set out to distinguish himself as a peacemaker. But his neglect of the navy meant European powers mostly ignored him, while English merchants and mariners condemned him for failing to stand up to Spain. His daughter, Elizabeth, married Frederick V, elector palatine, who became for a year King of Bohemia, where she was known as the Winter Queen. James was certainly in no position to extend help to them when they were driven out of Prague, but one advantage of this weakness was that England did not become involved in the Thirty Years War.

Under Buckingham's influence, James conceived the unpopular idea of marrying his son, Charles, to the Spanish infanta. Disguised as Jack and Tom Smith, Charles and Buckingham rode across France with the intention of bringing her back as Charles's wife. But when they arrived in Madrid, Charles offended the Spaniards by jumping over the infanta's garden wall in an attempt to take her by surprise. James meanwhile wrote lovelorn letters to his 'sweet boys' who might 'never look to see your old dad again'. The marriage did not come off, for the Spaniards made unacceptable demands for the suspension of laws against English Catholics. But Charles instead married Henrietta Maria, sister of Louis XIII of France: a match that was to prove just as unpopular.

James's powers were by now failing, and after a last warning to Charles about the growing power of the House of Commons, he died. It has been said of this king that although he steered the ship of state straight for the rocks, he left his son to wreck it.

CHARLES I

1625–1649

Charles I was a shy but intransigent king. He failed as a statesman and war leader, and after letting down some of his most devoted servants, had his head chopped off. But it is impossible for any true cavalier to avoid, on coming across one of Anthony Van Dyck's portraits, a stab of loyalty towards this most elegant monarch.

The struggle in which his reign culminated gave rise to the most memorable summary in an English history book: it was, the authors of 1066 and All That said, between 'the Cavaliers (Wrong but Wromantic) and the Roundheads (Right but Repulsive)'. To this day, the English are divided, by temperament, into Cavaliers and Roundheads.

Charles was born in 1600 in Dunfermline Palace, near Edinburgh. He was the second son of James VI of Scotland, who was soon to go south and rule as James I of England. When Charles was twelve, his beloved older brother, Henry, died, and he became heir to the throne. He grew to the modest height of five feet four inches, was known to his father as 'Baby Charles' and suffered from a lifelong stutter. As a child he had been over-shadowed by his more glamorous brother, and he continued to feel a lack of faith in his own abilities, for which he compensated by an inflexible belief in the divine right of kings, in which everyone around him was expected to believe too.

His wife, Henrietta Maria, the high-spirited, headstrong sixteen-year-old sister of the King of France, was affronted by the amount of time her husband spent with the young Duke of Buckingham, and refused point-blank to attend the joint corona-tion which had been arranged: she said that as a Roman Catholic, it was out of the question for her to be crowned by a Protestant bishop. Her popularity never recovered, especially as she remained ostentatiously Catholic. At the end of the coronation service, London was shaken by an earthquake, and Charles burst into tears.

For the first years of his reign, he continued to rely heavily on his father's favourite, Buckingham. In the 1620s Buckingham strove to set himself up as a Protestant hero, and led various naval expeditions, including an attempt to rescue the French Protestants in La Rochelle. All were miserable failures, for forces of the neces-sary quality could not simply be improvised. Few people apart from Charles felt saddened by Buckingham's assassination in Portsmouth in 1628 while preparing another expedition. The king's relations with his young wife now improved: they became very fond of each other and had nine children, of whom five, including the future Charles II and James II, survived to adulthood. And Charles amassed the wonderful collection of pictures, later sold by the Puritans, which established him as the pre-eminent collector in English royal history.

The heavy expense of his inglorious wars made relations with Parliament very much more difficult. Charles found himself obliged to resort to forced loans and other detested measures. In 1628, Parliament pressurised him into signing the Petition of Right, which stated that there could be no forced loans without parliamentary consent, no imprisonment without cause being shown, and no martial law or billeting of soldiers in private houses.

The next year, Charles resolved – after further ructions including the holding down of the Commons Speaker and locking of the doors while motions attacking Crown policy were passed – to rule without Parliament: a course he managed to keep to for the next eleven years. To raise money, he levied Ship Money even on inland towns. John Hampden, a wealthy parliamentarian of ancient family and moderate inclinations, challenged in the courts his right to do so. Hampden lost the case but clarified the issue: if royal tyranny was to be prevented, Parliament had to assert control of taxation.

In his choice of subordinates, Charles valued ruthless consistency above tact. Sir Thomas Wentworth, later ennobled as Earl of Strafford, was sent to Ireland, where he instituted the merciless programme of administrative reform known to him by the term 'Thorough'. His nickname among his opponents was Black Tom Tyrant.

Charles appointed William Laud, a gifted High Church scholar, as Archbishop of Canterbury. James I would never have done this, for as he himself said: 'I keep Laud back from all place of rule and authority, because I find that he hath a restless spirit, and cannot see when things are well but loves to toss and change, and to bring things to a pitch of reformation floating in his own brain.' Elizabeth I would have known at once that Laud's urge not just to preach but to enforce conformity was dangerous.

But to Charles, Laud's uncompromising approach was just what was needed. The archbishop insisted on a greater degree of ritual than the Puritans could bear: some of them emigrated, but many others remained in a growing state of discontent. There was widespread anger when three outspoken Puritans were punished by having their ears chopped off. The most notorious of the three, William Prynne, had published a 1,000-page condemnation of the 'sin' of acting: this included an index reference to 'women actors, notorious whores', which was taken as a direct attack on Henrietta Maria, who was fond of taking part in amateur theatricals.

Worse followed in Scotland, where Charles on Laud's advice ordered the use of a prayer book modelled on the one in use in the Church of England. In St Giles's Church in Edinburgh, where the book was first used in July 1637, there was a riot. A market trader called Jenny Geddes is said to have started it by hurling her stool at the clergyman reading the service. Scots came together to sign a Covenant in which they swore to defend their Kirk and resist popery.

A prudent king would have seen that he had completely misjudged the mood of his subjects north of the border, and would have taken steps to conciliate the Covenanters. Charles said he would 'rather die than yield to their impertinent and damnable demands'. He raised an army of reluctant troops, and summoned Strafford from Ireland to be his right-hand man.

Strafford advised Charles to summon a Parliament, so that it could supply the money needed to subdue the Scots. The Short Parliament met in April 1640, demanded the redress of eleven years' pent-up grievances before it would vote any money for Charles, and was swiftly dismissed. The king proposed to wage war on the Scots without parliamentary support. But the Scots instead waged war on him, bypassing the border fortress of Berwick-upon-Tweed, capturing Newcastle and advancing as far south as Yorkshire.

Charles was forced to summon what became known as the Long Parliament, which met in November 1640 and continued in various forms for the next twenty years. Under the able leadership of John Pym, MPs attacked almost every aspect of Charles's reign. They accused Strafford of treason, and in particular of planning to use Irish troops to oppress England. Charles assured Strafford he would not allow him to be executed, but became worried for the safety of the royal family, and in May 1641 signed the death warrant: a deep blot on the king's conscience. Laud too was imprisoned and charged, but not executed until 1645.

In January 1642, Charles tried to seize the initiative. Convinced that five MPs, including Pym and Hampden, were stirring up opposition to him everywhere from Scotland to London, he entered the Commons – the only king to do so – and attempted to arrest them. But the Five Members, as they became known, were forewarned, and had already escaped by boat to the City of London, where they knew they would be safe. 'I see the birds have flown,' Charles said, before asking the Speaker, William Lenthall, whether he could spot any of the five.

Lenthall knelt in front of the king and uttered what became the classic expression of the right of the Commons to govern itself rather than take instructions from the executive: 'May it please Your Majesty, I have neither eyes to see nor tongue to speak in this place, but as the House is pleased to direct me, whose servant I am here.'

Charles had failed to impose himself on Parliament, and a few days later left London. The issue would now be decided by war, but already the king was at a disadvantage: he had left behind him the richest city in England, and his enemies had command of the seas too. The first pitched battle, at Edgehill in October 1642, was inconclusive, and he set up his headquarters at Oxford.

The king's most gifted commander was his nephew, Prince Rupert of the Rhine. But even he could not defy indefinitely the austere and conscientious professionalism of the New Model Army, formed at the start of 1645 by Sir Thomas Fairfax and Oliver Cromwell, which in June that year crushed the Royalists at the Battle of Naseby. Charles surrendered himself to the Scots, with whom he tried to do a deal, but they in due course handed him over to Parliament, from which the New Model Army seized control of him in an operation led by Cornet Joyce. Cromwell defeated the Scots, who had belatedly mounted an invasion in support of the king.

The only way in which Charles could save himself was by reaching a sensible compromise with his adversaries. They, after all, were deeply split into various religious and political factions, and most of them were also deeply reluctant to have him put to death. For his enemies, he remained an inconveniently popular figure. But Charles could never bring himself to admit that he should be aiming for a lasting peace with the more conservative-minded of his opponents, who were no more minded than he was to take up the strange new egalitarian ideas which were emerging in some of the lower reaches of society.

Instead the king wriggled, prevaricated, escaped, was recaptured, and throughout demonstrated his complete untrustworthiness. In true Stuart style, he acknowledged no obligation to give up his right to conduct himself as he saw fit.

The Army lost patience both with Charles and with Parliament, which in December 1648 it subjected to Pride's Purge, named after Colonel Pride, the officer who carried it out. This left only seventy-five MPs, who became known as the Rump Parliament, with a much larger number arrested or excluded. The Army instructed the Rump to set up a High Court of Justice to try Charles for treason.

The king refused to recognise the court. It consisted of 135 commissioners, or judges, of whom only sixty-eight turned up to Westminster Hall to try him, and of these only fifty-nine signed his death warrant, so one might say the court even refused to recognise itself.

Charles was executed on 30 January 1649, on a scaffold erected outside the Banqueting House in Whitehall. As it was a cold morning, he wore two shirts for the walk across the park from St James's Palace, so that he would not shiver with cold, and be thought to tremble with fear.

He showed no fear. At the end, his stutter fell away, and he spoke from the heart in defence of the beliefs which prevented him being an effective negotiator, or understanding the strange new currents of opinion that were stirring. His own ideals were not yet anachronistic, and were held every bit as sincerely as his opponents'. He began by observing that 'an unjust Sentence that I suffered for to take effect, is punished now by an unjust Sentence upon me': a reference to his betrayal almost eight years before of Strafford. Charles proceeded to point out the illegality of what was happening, and to present himself as the guarantor of his people's freedom:

> As to the King, the Laws of the Land will clearly instruct you for that. For the People; and truly I desire their Liberty and Freedom, as much as anybody: but I must tell you that

their Liberty and Freedom consists in having the Government of those Laws by which their lives and their goods may be most their own; 'tis not for having a share in Government; Sirs, that is nothing pertaining to 'em. A Subject and a Sovereign are clean different things . . . if I would have given way to an arbitrary way, for to have all Laws changed according to the Power of the Sword, I needed not to have come here; and therefore I tell you (and I pray God it be not laid to your charge) that I am the Martyr of the People.

As Charles's head was severed from his shoulders, the watching crowd let out a deep groan. An equestrian statue of this king stands today on the southern edge of Trafalgar Square, still pointing down Whitehall towards the spot where he died. It is perhaps the most perfectly proportioned statue in London, and quite often it is adorned with flowers.

THE INTERREGNUM
1649–1660

Oliver Cromwell declined two invitations to have himself crowned as king. In 1653 he was instead installed as Lord Protector. The French ambassador remarked with scornful amusement that the procession through London celebrating this event occurred 'with all the state and dignity of a sovereign, no difference, the same bowing and scraping, the same ambassadors, the same decorations, the same trumpeting and magnificence'.

As a military leader, Cromwell still knew how to carry all before him: with ruthless efficiency he subdued Ireland and defeated the Scots, who had formed an alliance with Charles I's son and heir. Partly in order to give the navy something to do, Cromwell also defeated the Dutch and the Spanish. England's power had seldom been greater.

But how was England to be governed? This question even the great Cromwell could not answer. Parliament had declared a Commonwealth, or republic, but soon asked him to become king, which would mean his powers were more limited than as Protector. The Army rejected this plan: it had not overthrown the Stuarts in order to create a dynasty of Cromwells.

There was a ferment of political ideas at this time, many of them astonishingly radical, and of political writing, some of it by great men, including John Milton and Thomas Hobbes. But there were far too many dissensions to create a republic which was seen as legitimate and could sustain itself. Legitimacy was still conferred by monarchy. In 1658, when Cromwell unexpectedly fell ill, he nominated his son Richard as his successor. Richard soon recognised that he was unable to fill his father's shoes, and stood aside. The way was open for the Stuarts to return.

CHARLES II
1660–1685

harles II is the wittiest monarch in English history. He was courageous, tolerant, lazy, duplicitous and pleasure-loving: his return in 1660 from exile inaugurated the most conspicuous change in manners, from extreme puritanism to unbridled licentiousness, this country has ever seen. But he conducted the restoration of the Stuart dynasty with such tact, and rode every later crisis with such skill, that he was never in serious danger of being unseated.

He was born in 1630, the oldest surviving child of Charles I and his French queen, Henrietta Maria. For a few years he knew the sweetness of life before the civil war, but at the age of twelve he was nearly captured at the Battle of Edgehill, and he spent several years of the conflict at his father's side before being forced to flee across the Channel.

When Charles was eighteen, and living in Holland, his father was executed. The next year, Charles landed in Scotland, where he was crowned King of Scots at Scone, after which he played a game of golf. He raised an army of 10,000 men and marched south, but the English at this time regarded the Scots as barbarians, and had no desire to make common cause with them. Cromwell caught up with the invaders at Worcester and inflicted a decisive defeat.

Charles, who had fought bravely, was now a fugitive with a £1,000 price on his head, and death as the penalty for anyone who helped him. The five Penderel brothers, Catholics from Boscobel, in Shropshire, nevertheless disguised him as a wood cutter, and hid him for a day in what became known as the Royal Oak, through whose branches he saw the soldiers searching for him. Without the help of the Catholic underground, skilled in secret operations, he would have had very little chance.

For six weeks, Charles was on the run. For part of the time he was able to travel on the same horse as a woman, Jane Lane, whose servant he pretended to be. He travelled over 600 miles from safe house to safe house, and had many narrow escapes, for he was six feet two inches tall and despite his various disguises and his gifts as an actor, was quite often recognised.

But he kept his nerve, no one turned him in, and after a failed attempt to set sail from Lyme Regis, in Dorset, he was at last able to get a boat from Shoreham, in Sussex, to France. When he became king, he had an exceptional knowledge, for a monarch, of what it was like to live among his own people. The Stuarts often omitted to look after those with a claim on their gratitude. But Charles did take care, once he could, to help those who had helped him (the Penderels and their descendants got pensions), and told the whole story to Samuel Pepys, who wrote it down.

While Cromwell lived, there was scant chance of Charles regaining his throne. But in 1658, that invincible leader died, and the situation became much more promising. The English were weary of the life-denying severities which had been imposed on them in the name of extreme Protestantism, including the banning of traditional sports, plays and Christmas festivities. In Macaulay's phrase, 'The Puritan hated bearbaiting, not because it gave pain to the bear, but because it gave pleasure to the spectators.'

At the beginning of 1660, the astute and secretive General Monck marched south from Scotland with a powerful army. The Long Parliament of 1640 now dissolved itself and was succeeded by the Convention Parliament. Charles wrote from Holland offering his help: in what became known as the Declaration of Breda, he offered a general pardon, except to the regicides who had signed his father's death warrant, and in matters of religion, promised 'liberty to tender consciences'.

In May 1660, the king was welcomed with joy to London. A dozen regicides were put to death, but there was no general attempt to take revenge on the Roundheads. Parliament was unfortunately less inclined than Charles himself to toleration in matters of religion: in 1662, it passed the Act of Uniformity, which was the Cavaliers' revenge on Roundheads who dissented from the Church of England. The Prayer Book was restored, about 2,000 clergy who refused to use it were turned out of their places without compensation, and under the Conventicle Act, prison and transportation were imposed on Dissenters.

The New Model Army was paid off: the English had a deep

distrust of standing armies which might be used as instruments of tyranny. The Coldstream Guards, raised by Monck before he crossed the Tweed into England, was one of the few regiments to survive this cull. But investment was made, as far as means permitted, in the Royal Navy. As Charles himself recognised, 'It is upon the Navy under the Providence of God that the safety, honour and welfare of this Realm do chiefly depend.'

Charles married Catherine of Braganza, a Portuguese princess who unfortunately turned out to be barren. His mistresses included Lucy Walters, Barbara Villiers (created Duchess of Cleveland), Louise de Kéroualle (created Duchess of Portsmouth) and the actress Nell Gwyn. They quite often bore him children, on whom it pleased him to confer dukedoms, so that some of the most illustrious members of the English and Scottish peerage are descended from Charles II's bastards.

Bishop Burnet wrote of Charles II: 'He once said to myself, he was no atheist, but he could not think God would make a man miserable only for taking a little pleasure out of the way.' He is known as the Merry Monarch: a term coined by Lord Rochester, a brilliant and even by modern standards obscene poet who was often banished from court for his rudeness at the expense of the king, and as often allowed back, for Charles was no prude, and enjoyed a joke even at his own expense.

Here is the bulk of Rochester's 'A Satire on Charles II'. It conveys the spirit in which that king's court – the last brilliant and fashionable court in English history – was conducted, but readers who are dismayed by earthy language should skip to the next page.

> I' th' isle of Britain, long since famous grown
> For breeding the best cunts in Christendom,
> There reigns, and oh! long may he reign and thrive,

The easiest King and best-bred man alive.
Him no ambition moves to get renown
Like the French fool, that wanders up and down
Starving his people, hazarding his crown.
Peace is his aim, his gentleness is such,
And love he loves, for he loves fucking much.
Nor are his high desires above his strength;
His sceptre and his prick are of a length;
And she may sway the one who plays with th'other,
And make him little wiser than his brother.
Poor prince! thy prick, like thy buffoons at Court,
Will govern thee because it makes thee sport.
'Tis sure the sauciest prick that e'er did swive,
The proudest, peremptoriest prick alive.
Though safety, law, religion, life lay on 't,
'Twould break through all to make its way to cunt.
Restless he rolls about from whore to whore,
A merry monarch, scandalous and poor.

The brother is the future James II, while the French fool is Charles's first cousin, Louis XIV. Charles, it should be added, had many other interests too: he gave his blessing to the founding of the Royal Society, for the study of science.

In 1665, London was afflicted by the Great Plague, and in 1666 by the Great Fire, where Charles took command and ordered the demolition of houses to stop the spread of the conflagration. These disasters were followed in 1667 by the audacious and humiliating Dutch raid on the Medway, where English warships were destroyed at anchor. The enemy's guns could be heard in London, and people began to think things might, after all, have been better in Cromwell's time, when the Royal Navy won famous victories under Admiral Blake. The king, it was said, 'minds nothing but his lust'.

Charles responded, somewhat unfairly, by dropping his chief minister, Edward Hyde, Earl of Clarendon, who had followed him into exile, had helped to ensure the success of the Restoration, and had opposed the war with the Dutch. Clarendon was perhaps too inclined to give honest advice, and did not hide his disapproval of the king's licentiousness. He was replaced by a rackety group of ministers, known collectively as the Cabal. Charles soon entered into a secret treaty with Louis XIV, who paid him a pension and hoped to turn England into a subservient and in due course Catholic country, which would help in the dismemberment of Protestant Holland.

Holland undermined this plan by refusing to be dismembered: instead, under the leadership of William of Orange, it stopped the French invasion by opening the dykes. And in England, Parliament grew increasingly suspicious of Charles's papist tendencies. In 1673, he ran out of money and was forced to agree to the Test Act, which excluded Catholics from office. The alarming discovery was made that the king's own brother, and heir, James, Duke of York, had converted to Catholicism.

Charles changed tack: as he himself said, he did not wish 'to go on his travels again'. He adopted an altogether more Anglican tone, which helped him to survive the febrile atmosphere of his final years, when the English were only too ready to believe in Catholic plots to subvert and subjugate them. The king managed to resist attempts to exclude his brother from the succession. James on one occasion warned him not to go for a walk without guards, to which Charles replied, 'You may depend upon it that nobody will ever think of killing me to make you king.'

Of a certain preacher and his congregation, Charles remarked, 'His nonsense suits their nonsense.' On his deathbed, Charles's thoughts turned to one of his mistresses, the actress Nell Gwyn, and he said: 'Do not let poor Nelly starve.' He also apologised for being 'an unconscionable time dying'. Here was a king who possessed to the end what Richard Ollard has called 'his most universally endearing characteristic – the ability to stand outside himself and offer polite, amused comments on what he saw'. And it was Father Huddleston, a priest who had helped him when he was on the run, who at the end received the king into the Catholic Church.

On another occasion, Charles remarked that Presbyterianism is 'not a religion for gentlemen'. Charles was a gentlemanly king. His manners were so charming, and his self-possession so complete, that most people forgave him his weaknesses of the flesh, or indeed admired him for them.

JAMES II
1685–1688

James II was a pious, lustful, lugubrious, arrogant, ill-judging monarch. Although he possessed military and administrative ability, he never grasped the need to fit in with his subjects. He believed God was on his side, so they should fit in with him. Unfortunately for James, although he looked handsome enough, his personality discouraged people from remaining loyal to him. Nell Gwyn called him 'dismal Jimmy'. His older brother, Charles II, teased him for having such ugly mistresses, one of whom, Catherine Sedley, admitted finding James's choice of her incomprehensible: 'It cannot be my beauty, for he must see that I have none; and it cannot be my wit, for he has not enough himself to know that I have any.'

More dangerous than his choice of women was his choice of religion. While still in his thirties, James converted to Roman Catholicism. Charles made a joke about this: he said the ugly mistresses must be a penance imposed by his brother's confessor. But James brought to religion his usual inflexible seriousness. As he himself said: 'My principles do not allow me to dissimulate my religion.' He also said: 'I cannot resolve to do evil that good may come of it.' It is scarcely surprising that he could not manage the politics of kingship.

Yet in 1685, when at the age of fifty-two he succeeded his brother on the throne, he seemed to be in a position of unassailable strength. He summoned a Parliament and promised: 'I shall always take care to defend and support the Church of England.' The Tory squires who dominated Parliament took him at his word. They were ardent royalists, and in James they thought they were welcoming a more hard-working, sober and economical king than Charles had been. They proved their loyalty by granting James a higher income than a Stuart monarch had ever received.

Soon after James became king, his nephew the Duke of Monmouth, a bastard son of Charles II, led a rebellion in the West Country. It was crushed by James's army at the Battle of Sedgemoor. Monmouth fled disguised as a peasant, was found hiding in a ditch, pleaded with James for his life and was executed. Contemporaries were impressed by the harshness with which Judge Jeffreys, urged on by the king, punished many other rebels. They were hanged, their bodies left dangling from gibbets along the roads of Wessex, or else they were transported to the West Indies.

James was emboldened by this success to embark on the Romanisation of England. One of his instruments was to be his standing army of 40,000 men. He replaced its officers with Roman Catholics, of whom he could not find enough in England, so he sent to Ireland for more.

The king affronted the Tory squires by appointing Roman Catholics as Justices of the Peace and to other offices usually held by Anglicans. When Parliament indicated that it would not repeal the Test Act, which since 1673 had excluded Roman Catholics from public office, James got round this by prevailing on the judiciary to allow him to override the Act whenever he wished. The Tories began to realise that James, far from being their friend, was their mortal enemy.

There could scarcely have been a worse moment to attempt this forced Romanisation. France's Protestants, the Huguenots, were suffering a ferocious persecution which prompted many of them to flee to London. Louis XIV demonstrated that under a Catholic monarch, Protestants could expect to be treated as slaves, and James was all too clearly modelling himself on Louis. Hatred of popery reached new heights among Protestants of every description.

But at least James's heirs were Protestant: Mary and Anne, only survivors of the eight children born to Anne Hyde, his first wife, who had herself died in 1671. There was yet hope that England would be delivered from tyranny by James's death, which would lead to the succession of Mary and her unquestionably Protestant husband, William of Orange.

It was true that James had married for a second time, to a Roman Catholic, Mary of Modena. She was a beautiful girl of fifteen, and screamed for forty-eight hours on hearing of the husband, twenty-five years older than herself, who was to be hers. But none of her six pregnancies had produced a child who survived more than four years.

In September 1687, James rode to St Winefride's Well in Wales to pray for a son. His prayers were answered: within a fortnight Mary of Modena was pregnant. In June 1688, she gave birth in a stuffy room, crowded with the dozens of dignitaries who were supposed to witness a royal birth. The baby was hurried away to an airier room nearby and its sex proclaimed – a boy! a boy! – before the official witnesses could see if this was so.

The rumour spread that the baby had been smuggled into the room in a warming pan, to replace a royal child who had been stillborn. Once this story was abroad, it proved impossible to dispel. Many people were determined to believe a trick had been played in order to provide James with a Catholic son who would take precedence over his daughters.

In a further insult to his subjects, the king invited the Pope to be the boy's godfather. James believed he had not just the right but the power to defy popular feeling. He instructed the clergy to read from their pulpits the Declaration of Indulgence, which suspended the laws against Roman Catholics and Dissenters. Seven bishops led the resistance to this measure. They were placed on trial and on 30 June 1688 were acquitted amid scenes of jubilation.

That night, an invitation to William of Orange to invade England was signed by six leading noblemen and the Bishop of London. James now committed a further miscalculation: at the very moment when he needed the help of Louis XIV he publicly refused it. Too late he feared antagonising the English. William could now invade without fearing that Louis would hasten to rescue James.

The first time William set out from Holland, he was blown back to shore. By November 1688, James was sure he would not come: the weather was too bad. But William set out again, and 'the Protestant wind' blew him down the Channel and along the south coast of England. James's admiral, who feared a mutiny among his Protestant sailors, took care not to attack him. William landed at Torbay, in Devon, with an army of 15,000. James advanced with his standing army of 40,000 men, which had been stationed on Hounslow Heath in order to intimidate London.

The king – for James was still the lawful king – got as far as Salisbury, where he found himself incapacitated by nosebleeds. Some have suggested he was suffering from syphilis, but it seems more likely that he was crushed by what seemed to him an unbearable choice: to advance and slaughter his daughter's husband, or retreat and lose his kingdom.

While James suffered a nervous breakdown and returned to London, his army started to disintegrate. One of the first defectors was John Churchill, son of Sir Winston Churchill and brother of Arabella Churchill, a woman who despite being 'nothing but skin and bone' had been one of James's early mistresses and borne him four children. James had just promoted John Churchill to the rank of lieutenant general, but Churchill, at the head of 400 officers and men, now deserted him in his hour of need. But for this astute and timely act, he would never have become, as Duke of Marlborough, one of Britain's greatest soldiers. In the 1930s, another Winston Churchill composed a long and eloquent biography of his ancestor in which he attempted, not quite successfully, to defend him against the charge of treachery.

William advanced without opposition on London. James despaired of his cause, threw the Great Seal, needed to ratify England's laws, into the Thames, and fled to Faversham, in Kent, where he boarded a boat for France but got stuck on a sandbank. He was captured and had smoke blown in his face by Kentish fishermen, but was proud to have concealed his coronation ring in his drawers.

To William's consternation, James was brought back to Whitehall. William, who had no other way to oust his father-in-law, prevailed on him once more to flee, this time accompanied by the Duke of Berwick, one of James's children by Arabella Churchill. On board ship they ate bacon out of an old frying pan with a hole in it, and on Christmas Day 1688 they landed in France.

Bishop Burnet, an early supporter of William of Orange, wrote of the downfall of James: 'One of the strangest catastrophes that is in any history. A great king, with strong armies and mighty fleets, a great treasure and powerful allies, fell all at once, and his whole strength, like a spider's web, was . . . irrecoverably broken at a touch.'

The following year James attempted via Ireland to regain his throne, but in 1690 he was defeated by William at the Battle of the Boyne. William forbade pursuit, for the last thing he wanted was to recapture his father-in-law.

A grand French lady said of the exiled James: 'To tell the truth, our good King James is a brave and honest man, but the silliest I have ever seen in my life; a child of seven would not make such crass mistakes as he does. Piety makes people outrageously stupid.'

James lost his crown by pursuing a course of such conscientious foolhardiness that he united the English nation against himself. At the French court he was regarded as a bore, and people avoided him. He became ever more devout, and after his death in 1701 narrowly missed being made a saint.

WILLIAM III & MARY II

1689–1702

William III is one of the greatest kings of England, and one of the least remembered. No one could have been more skilful at deposing James II, or at negotiating the terms for a monarchy more acceptable to Parliament. But even in his lifetime, this bold, cold, asthmatic Dutchman was not popular. Only in Northern Ireland is he remembered as a hero, the victor of the Battle of the Boyne. Loyalists still mark their territory by painting murals of King Billy, mounted on a white horse which often proves difficult to draw.

William was born in November 1650 in The Hague. His mother, Mary Stuart, was a daughter of Charles I and wished to call him Charles, but the Dutch side of the family insisted on William, in memory of his father, who died of smallpox shortly before the birth. This father was William II, Prince of Orange, in southern France, and Stadtholder, or ruler, of the United Provinces, as Holland and the rest of the Netherlands were then known.

The son had a regal upbringing: his christening robe was trimmed with ermine, at the age of two and a half he had his own court, at four he made public appearances and at nine he carried out official duties on his own. He was fluent in French, Dutch, German and Spanish, and learned some English from his mother. She died in 1660, the year his uncle, Charles II, was restored to the throne.

William was now on his own, which helped explain his reserved and self-controlled manner. He was small and physically unimpressive, with a hooked nose, hunched back and permanent cough. From the age of eighteen, his entire life was spent in the struggle to defend Holland against Louis XIV. This seemed like a fight William could not win. France had 20 million inhabitants; Holland had 2 million.

But in battle, William lost his reserve, and even his asthma improved. His courage was beyond reproach. He led by example, wearing always his Order of the Garter, and being wounded many times. Condé, one of the great French generals, said of him: 'He acted in all respects like an old captain, except in venturing his life too much, like a young one.'

William knew that Holland must find an ally, and that the obvious one was England, her commercial rival. In 1670, he visited England. He disapproved of Charles II's endless feasting. But his uncle managed to get him drunk, after which he was found climbing into the apartments of the maids of honour. On returning home, William only managed to save Holland by opening the dykes.

In 1677, he returned to London and succeeded in marrying Mary, older daughter and heir of James, Duke of York, who was later to become James II. Mary was fifteen years old, attractive, fashionable and tall: five feet eleven inches to his five feet seven. On learning that she was to marry William, who was twenty-seven, she wept for a day and a half. Bishop Burnet said of the bridegroom: 'He spoke little and very slowly, and with a disgusting dryness.'

After the marriage, Charles II drew the curtains round their marriage bed with the words: 'Now nephew, to your work! Hey! St George for England!'

But William and Mary came to love each other. She was popular in Holland, and liked the spotless Dutch houses, so different from what she had known in Whitehall. She and William enjoyed gardening. He saw to the fountains, she to the flowers. Her deep regret was that she was unable to conceive a child. After 1685, when Charles II died and her father succeeded him as James II, she was the heir to the English throne.

William waited. He knew he could be the Protestant king who saved England from papist tyranny (as it was seen by most English people). He sent his envoy, Everard van Weede van Dijkvelt, to London, seemingly to assure James of his support, but actually to assess the level of discontent, and to make contact with those who might decide to rebel.

The decisive year was 1688. By April, William had resolved to attempt an invasion. In June, when opposition to James reached its height, he arranged for himself to be invited to invade.

Louis XIV, who perhaps believed William's invasion would end, like the Spanish Armada, in disaster, very obligingly sent the French fleet to the Mediterranean, and the French army, which usually threatened Holland, to the Rhineland.

In November 1688, William's fleet of 225 vessels sailed down the Channel. Its banners proclaimed 'For Religion and Liberty'. William himself declared: 'This our expedition is intended for no other design than to have a free and lawful Parliament assembled as soon as possible.' This was nonsense, but at least it showed that he understood the anger caused by James's attempts to subvert Parliament.

William landed in Devon with a printing press as well as an army. His grasp of the need to present himself as a reasonable king for a reasonable people was as strong as James's was defective. He told his men they must pay for all provisions. No notables joined him at once, but William gave them time. After twelve days, they started to come in, and when James retreated without giving battle, and William moved on London, the trickle turned to a flood. In December 1688, James was prevailed upon to flee to France. It is hard to see what otherwise could have been done with him: execution seemed out of the question, and to have him languishing in prison would not have been satisfactory.

In January 1689, an election was called, and William withdrew his troops from all parliamentary boroughs. This behaviour contrasted most favourably with James, who attempted to fix elections by ousting local worthies. On 22 January, the Convention Parliament met: 'Convention' because it had not been summoned by the king.

William warned Parliament: 'I have not come over to establish a republic or be a Duke of Venice.' In other words, he was determined to be monarch, either in his own right or through Mary, who now returned from Holland. She was delighted to be home, and was thought to have shown too great a joy in taking over the apartments in the Palace of Whitehall of her stepmother, Mary of Modena.

On 13 February, a Declaration of Rights was read out to William and Mary, who were then offered the joint crown. This was a typical English fudge: it was not clear if the offer of the crown was conditional on William and Mary's agreement to the Declaration of Rights, or if that document amounted, like a Norman coronation charter, to no more than a statement of intent by the monarchs themselves.

But the Declaration of Rights, incorporated at the end of 1689 into the Bill of Rights, became entrenched constitutional practice. The crown could not tax without Parliament's consent or interfere in parliamentary elections. From that day to this, Parliament has met every year, and no outside power has been able to interfere in its debates.

It is not the intention, in this book, to sound the triumphalist note struck by some Whig historians, who trace an unbroken story of progress from the Glorious Revolution of 1688, or even from Magna Carta in 1215. The aim here is to draw brief lives of our monarchs. Thanks in part to William III, they would from now on be constitutional monarchs. Parliament decided that James II, by fleeing, had abdicated, and that Roman Catholics were excluded from the throne. Jacobites – who supported the claims of James II and his descendants – could still believe in the divine right of kings. Supporters of William III could not.

James attempted, with French help, to regain his throne via Ireland. His decisive engagement with William occurred at the Battle of the Boyne in July 1690. At the start of the battle, William was grazed by a cannonball and knocked off his horse. He remounted and rode along his battle line, waving his sword to demonstrate that he was unhurt. The Dutch Blue Guards led the attack across the River Boyne, with heavy casualties. William himself led a cavalry crossing lower down. Many of James's followers were disgusted by the former king's poor leadership, and by his decision after the battle to return to France rather than continue the fight.

From 1691 to 1697, William spent each campaign season abroad, fighting the French. Mary acted as regent while he was away. 'It breaks my brains,' she said. In December 1694, she died of smallpox at the age of thirty-two. William, who had installed his camp bed in her sickroom, was distraught. He even dismissed his mistress, Betty Villiers.

The foundation of the Bank of England in 1694 gave the English government access to cheap credit: an advantage the French did not possess. In 1697, at the Peace of Ryswick, Louis XIV gave up all recent gains and acknowledged William as King of England. Parliament promptly cut the size of the army to a mere 7,000 men, leading William to remark: 'Parliament did in a day what Louis XIV had been unable to do in eight years.' His cold manner, reliance on Dutch friends and advisers, and determination to spend huge sums on the war against France, made him unloved.

On 21 February 1702, William was injured when his horse stumbled on a molehill at Hampton Court, and on 8 March he died at Kensington Palace, which with Mary he had turned into a royal residence. He was found to have her ring and a lock of her hair in a locket round his neck. The Jacobites toasted 'the little gentleman in black velvet' who had killed the man they were unable to kill.

ANNE

1702–1714

Queen Anne was the last and least regal of the Stuarts, and in some respects the most astute. She was the younger daughter of James II and of his first wife, Anne Hyde. This makes her one of our few monarchs to have had a commoner as a parent: a characteristic she shares with William the Conqueror.

In November 1688, Anne deserted her father and joined the invasion led by William of Orange, who was married to her sister, Mary. For James, this was a shattering blow: 'Even my children have deserted me.' But for Anne, it was the right decision. She was a Protestant, a loyal member of the Church of England, and Parliament was determined that the country should have a Protestant monarch who would uphold English liberties.

William and Mary had no children. Anne, by contrast, had no difficulty getting pregnant. She married Prince George of Denmark, often dismissed as the dullest royal consort in history: Charles II said he had tried him drunk and tried him sober, and there was nothing in him.

George was actually an amiable man who wanted a quiet life and was happy for his wife to be queen without him demanding a dominant role as William had done. Anne and George were devoted to each other. The irreparable sadness of their marriage was that although in sixteen years she had eighteen pregnancies, only five of their children were born alive, and four of those died in infancy. The longest-lived was the Duke of Gloucester, who died in 1700 at the age of eleven.

This unhappy event impelled Parliament to pass the Act of Settlement, which excluded all Catholic claimants to the throne, including James II's son, James Edward, usually known as the Old Pretender. When Anne died, the throne would instead pass to the House of Hanover, which was Protestant, and was descended in the female line from James I.

Anne's reign was marked by continental triumphs of a magnitude not seen since Agincourt. John Churchill, Duke of Marlborough, broke the dominance of France. His first and most astonishing victory, Blenheim, was fought on the Danube rather than the Rhine, and confirmed him as the greatest general England has produced. It was followed by Ramillies, Oudenarde and Malplaquet.

Historians often write of these victories as if they had nothing to do with the queen. But that is unfair. Anne knew the Churchills exceptionally well. As a child of six, she became great friends with Sarah Jennings, who at the age of fifteen married John Churchill, whose sister, Arabella, we last heard of as one of James II's mistresses.

William III mistrusted Churchill, who had deserted James II, and had done so at the moment when it would cause the greatest damage. Anne, who had made the same desertion, was less mistrustful, and made Churchill the captain general of her forces. This recruitment process was not in accordance with modern norms, but was abundantly justified by results.

Anne and Sarah were for a long time so close that they called each other Mrs Freeman and Mrs Morley: nicknames which enabled them to converse on terms of equality. In the 1690s, when Anne was on bad terms with William, to whom she referred as 'Mr Caliban', Sarah was her prop and stay.

Sarah wished to dominate Anne, and at length became insufferable. In 1708 she was replaced in the queen's affections by Abigail Hill, whom Sarah had introduced into royal service. Jonathan Swift, the author of *Gulliver's Travels*, observed that Anne 'had not a store of amity by her for more than one friend at a time'. Sarah was so angry that she put it about that Anne and Abigail were lesbians.

In January 1711, by which time the war with France was won, both the Churchills were dismissed. According to Walter Bagehot, 'Queen Anne was one of the smallest people ever set in a great place.' But the small person was in fact quite capable of standing up for herself.

One of the enduring achievements of Anne's reign was the Act of Union with Scotland. This took place not because the Scots and the English loved each other, but because they were on such bad terms. Statesmen on both sides saw that unless the two kingdoms were united, there would be recurrent war. Anne promoted the joining in 1707 of her two kingdoms into Great Britain, and was delighted when it happened. In 2014 the Scots voted in a referendum for the continuation of this Union.

For most of her life, Anne suffered from poor health. By 1702, she was already so lame that she had to be carried to her coronation in an open sedan chair. By 1714 she was grotesquely fat. She was known as 'Brandy Nan', in reference to her fondness for that drink. But she presided to the end at Cabinet meetings, and managed the strife between Whigs and Tories with more adroitness than is usually realised. The queen ensured that no powerful faction felt so permanently excluded from power that the Jacobites could take advantage of her death.

In 1711, Anne founded Ascot Racecourse. The first race for Her Majesty's Plate had seven runners. She was the last English monarch to touch for the king's evil, as scrofula was known, a custom found as far back as Edward the Confessor, who reigned from 1042 to 1066. The belief that the monarch had the miraculous power to heal people by touching them was slowly dying out, and became untenable once the Hanoverians took over in 1714. One of the people Anne touched was the three-year-old Samuel Johnson. She had an ordinariness, and a kindliness, which made her a comforting figure. She was devoted to the Church of England and set up Queen Anne's Bounty, a fund to augment the incomes of poor members of the clergy. She was probably the first of our monarchs to taste ice cream, for soon after she died, her confectioner, Mrs Mary Eales, published the first book in England to include a recipe for it.

GEORGE I

1714–1727

George I was fifty-four when he became king, and possessed few characteristics which were likely to endear him to his new subjects. He preferred to communicate in French, was fluent in German and Latin, but had neither the ability nor the desire to converse in English. He was fonder of living in Hanover, where he had succeeded his father as elector sixteen years before, and possessed autocratic powers. His main merit was that he was a Protestant, as laid down in the Act of Settlement of 1701, and could therefore be presumed to be a defender of his subjects' ancient liberties.

But George found it curious to live in a country where his word was not law, and he could not help himself to whatever he wanted:

The first morning after my arrival at St James's, I looked out of the window and saw a park with walls and a canal, and was told they were mine. The next day, the ranger of my park sent me a brace of fine carp out of my canal, and I was told I must give five guineas to the man for bringing me my own carp out of my own canal in my own park.

The king's followers nevertheless set out to help themselves to whatever they could lay their hands on in a country almost unbelievably rich compared to their own. He reached London with 'a flight of hungry Hanoverians' who, as Lord Mahon later put it, fell 'like so many famished vultures . . . with keen eyes and bended talons on the fruitful soil of England'.

Nor was George's treatment of the closest members of his family such as to suggest he was a particularly agreeable person. He married his first cousin, Sophia Dorothea, and had a son and a daughter with her. She was beautiful, lively, witty and accomplished, but soon George looked elsewhere.

She in her turn was attracted by a dashing young army officer, Philip von Königsmark. They planned to elope. Instead he was killed by the four guards who had been ordered to arrest him. At the age of twenty-eight, Sophia Dorothea was put in the castle of Ahlden, where she remained a prisoner until her death thirty-two years later. She never again saw her husband or her children. Her son was at this time eleven years old, her daughter seven.

The new king arrived in London without a wife, but with eighteen cooks, and two ugly and rapacious German mistresses whom he created the Countess of Darlington and the Duchess of Kendal. The former was very fat, so was nicknamed the Elephant, while the latter, unusually for George, was very tall and thin, so was known as the Maypole. It should not be supposed that these ladies had exclusive rights to the king. According to Lord Chesterfield, 'No woman came amiss to him, if she were only very willing and very fat.'

It should be said in George's defence that in taking mistresses, he was conforming to normal royal practice. When at George's coronation the Countess of Dorchester, who as Catherine Sedley had been James II's mistress, happened to bump into the Duchess of Portsmouth, who had been Charles II's mistress, and the Countess of Orkney, who was William III's mistress, she exclaimed: 'God! Who would have thought we three whores should meet here.'

If George had attempted to set a high moral tone, he would have been more out of place than he was. As it was, he was prudent enough to keep his head down, and possessed the unassailable merit of not being James II, or James's heir, the Old Pretender. In 1715, there was a Jacobite uprising, which was suppressed without much difficulty. The Old Pretender was not a formidable leader. And as even Bolingbroke, a Tory politician who had hoped to profit by allying himself with the Jacobites, was forced to admit, 'England would as soon have a Turk as a Roman Catholic for king.' The entire, and growing, business class supported the Hanoverians.

Only in Scotland could the Jacobites still count on substantial support, and hope in time to launch another rebellion. In northern Britain, they thought nothing of the 'wee wee German lairdie', as a later Jacobite song called George I. The new king's descent via his mother from James I did not, for the Jacobites, obscure the plain fact that he was not the rightful hereditary king, and had a worse claim to the throne than over fifty Roman Catholics whom Parliament had excluded from the succession.

Once the Fifteen, as the uprising was known, had been put down, George was determined to visit Hanover. But this raised the awkward question of what discretion to allow in his absence to his son, the Prince of Wales, whom he hated. Every Hanoverian king was on wretched terms with his son and heir. Instead of making his son regent, George revived the role of 'Guardian of the Realm', a title dating back to the Black Prince which carried much more limited powers.

In 1717, the mutual hatred of father and son produced one of the demeaning rows in which Hanoverian history is so rich. Caroline of Ansbach, the wife of the Prince of Wales, had borne him a second son. The prince invited George to be one godparent and the Bishop of Osnabruck the other. But George insisted that by English tradition the Lord Chamberlain, the Duke of Newcastle, must be the other godparent. George was well aware that the prince hated the duke.

After the christening, the prince shouted at the duke, 'Rascal, I shall find you out', meaning 'I'll be revenged on you'. But the prince's voice was thick with rage, and the duke thought he had shouted 'I shall fight you out'. The terrified duke rushed to tell George of this death threat. George flew into a rage, called the Cabinet together, and sent ministers to interrogate the prince, who in turn said the duke was a liar. Maddened by this slur on his minister, George ordered that the Prince of Wales and Caroline of Ansbach be placed under house arrest.

The prince, remembering his own mother's continuing imprisonment, which had already lasted for twenty-three years, did not regard this as an idle threat, and grew more conciliatory. The king was with difficulty persuaded not to lock up the heir to the throne. But George still banished the prince and Caroline from St James's Palace, while with characteristic malice retaining their children 'for education'.

The prince instead set up court at Leicester House, in what is now Leicester Square. This was far more amusing than King

George's court: George had no queen to help him to make things go, or indeed any desire to make them go himself.

The Princess of Wales was beautiful, clever and sweet-natured, and knew how to make life enjoyable. Her ability to combine elegance with earthiness was thoroughly eighteenth century. She had corresponded with Leibniz, a brilliant mathematician and philosopher who worked for forty years for the House of Hanover, but she also understood the value of prominent breasts, prominently displayed. Robert Walpole was among the out-of-favour politicians who congregated at Leicester House. It was said of her soirées: 'learned men and divines were intermixed with courtiers and ladies of the household: the conversation turned upon metaphysical subjects, blended with repartees, sallies of mirth, and the tittle-tattle of the drawing room'.

George I stopped attending Cabinet meetings, at which his son had previously acted as interpreter. But in the spring of 1720, Walpole achieved the unlikely feat of engineering a reconciliation between the king and the Prince of Wales. Walpole had a remarkable gift for making it worth people's while to do what he wanted them to do. He himself came back into the ministry as Paymaster General, an office of great profit to him.

Meanwhile the South Sea Bubble was swelling to grotesque size: a speculative venture in which otherwise sane individuals invested with manic enthusiasm in ventures which could never make money. There was one 'For the planting of mulberry trees and the breeding of silkworms in Chelsea Park', another 'For a wheel for perpetual motion', a third 'For carrying on an undertaking of great advantage; but nobody to know what it is'.

Everyone from the king down put money into these schemes, which ministers were also heavily involved in promoting, for the South Sea Company was supposed to take over part of the national debt. Great was the dismay when the bubble burst. George himself was affected by the disaster, and a number of his ministers were ruined, as were thousands of private individuals.

Walpole, who had managed by a mixture of luck and judgement to avoid losing money, rendered himself indispensable by shielding a number of his colleagues. From 1721, he was First Lord of the Treasury, or what later came to be called prime minister: an expression he himself would never have used, for it was meant derogatorily, to signify that he had accumulated too much power. Lord Chesterfield said of him: 'He was both the best Parliament-man, and the ablest manager of Parliament, that ever lived.'

George I lived in two rooms of St James's Palace, where he was looked after by two servants, Mohammed and Mustapha, whom he had captured as a young man while campaigning against the Turks. Apart from his mistresses, his chief recreation was cutting paper into patterns. He enjoyed music, and brought Handel to England, but was in other respects a philistine, and one with no royal manner. Lady Mary Wortley Montagu described him as 'an honest blockhead . . . more properly dull than lazy'. Late in his reign, he made himself more popular by taking an English mistress, Ann Brett. His command of the English language remained poor.

The king is said to have been disturbed by a prophecy that he would die soon after his imprisoned wife. She perished in November 1726. In June 1727, when George was on his way to Hanover, he died at Delden, in Holland. The night before, he had consumed an enormous meal, including a large number of melons. Even as he fell ill, he was desperate to get home, and according to Thackeray, 'thrust his livid head out of the coach-window, and gasped out "Osnaburg, Osnaburg!"'

The first of our Hanoverian kings was buried, appropriately enough, in Hanover. But a few yards from the British Museum, an idealised statue of him still stands, dressed as a Roman, on top of the steeple of St George's, Bloomsbury.

GEORGE II

1727–1760

On learning of George I's death, his minister, Sir Robert Walpole, galloped down the road from Chelsea to Richmond to inform the new king. George II was in bed with Queen Caroline, asleep after his dinner. He was forty-three years old, and was displeased to be woken. Half dressed, he received the news not merely with astonishment, but with disbelief: 'Dat is one big lie!'

As so often, George took time to comprehend what was going on. One feels, looking back at him, that although this dapper little man reigned for thirty-three years, he never quite connected with England. Like his father, whom he came increasingly to resemble, he did not hide his preference for Hanover. His wife, Caroline of Ansbach, was much quicker on the uptake, and more at home in her new country: she has been described (by Lucy Worsley) as 'the cleverest queen consort ever to sit on the throne of England'.

It was assumed that the new king would lose no time in getting rid of Walpole, whom he very much disliked. And this expectation was correct: the king informed Walpole that from now on, Sir Spencer Compton would be in charge. But on hearing of his sudden promotion, Compton burst into tears, and protested that he was not up to it.

Caroline explained to George that Walpole was, after all, indispensable, for he was the only man who could be relied upon to get money out of Parliament. The next day, Walpole was back in power. Gossips put it about that Walpole was the queen's lover. This was not true, but there was an affinity between them: a mutual pleasure in understanding how the world worked.

Walpole, who spent his life hiding a subtle intelligence behind the manners of a rustic Norfolk squire, said of the queen that he 'took the right sow by the ear'. He had very soon seen through George: 'The king is – for all his personal bravery – as great a political coward as ever wore a crown, and as much afraid to lose it.' George could be pushed around, and was pushed around.

The king comforted himself by leading a tediously regular life, including an appointment at nine each evening with his mistress, Henrietta Howard. If he was a few minutes early he would wait, walking up and down the gallery outside until the clock struck the hour. Meanwhile Walpole built Houghton Hall, a palatial house in Norfolk, and filled it with the best pictures money could buy: Titian, Rubens, Raphael, Rembrandt, Poussin. He refused a peerage, in order the better to control the Commons, the more disorderly of the two Houses of Parliament. His enemies raged in vain against his readiness to reward those close to him. A newspaper listed the offices which he and his family held:

First Lord of the Treasury, Mr Walpole. Chancellor of the Exchequer, Mr Walpole. Clerk of the Pells, Mr Walpole's son. Customs of London, second son of Mr Walpole, in Reversion [i.e. after the death of the previous holder, Walpole's cousin]. Secretary of the Treasury, Mr Walpole's brother. Postmaster General, Mr Walpole's brother. Secretary to Ireland, Mr Walpole's brother. Secretary to the Postmaster General, Mr Walpole's brother-in-law.

But thanks to Walpole, England too was growing richer. He avoided war, encouraged trade, lowered taxes, refrained from ambitious schemes of reform which might go wrong. He knew the value of tranquillity, of which England had known so little in the last century. As he said to the queen in 1734: 'Madam, there are fifty thousand men slain this year in Europe, and not one Englishman.' He loved hunting, the English substitute for war, and liked it to be known that he opened his letters from his gamekeeper before official dispatches. But he was also an able administrator, the best that the eighteenth century was to see.

It says much for Walpole's powers that despite keeping England at peace, he managed, with Caroline's help, to keep George II under control. For George was a soldier, who yearned for battles in which he could show off his undoubted bravery. As a young man, he had distinguished himself at the head of the Hanoverian troops in Marlborough's victory at Oudenarde. On high days and holidays, he would appear in the hat and coat he wore in that battle.

Caroline's admirable qualities did not include love of her oldest son, Frederick, who for fourteen years of his childhood had been left behind in Hanover. 'If I was to see him in hell,' she said, 'I should feel no more for him than I should for any other rogue that ever went there.' The king agreed, describing the Prince of Wales as 'the greatest beast, the greatest liar and the greatest fool in the world'.

In 1737, Caroline fell mortally ill. For as long as she could, she concealed her agonies from her husband, who was irritated by illness. She had tolerated all his faults, including his mistresses, about whom he confided in her. When he seduced a new one, the Countess von Walmoden, in Hanover in 1735, he wrote to Caroline: 'You must love the Walmoden, for she loves me.'

As Caroline lay dying, the depth of the king's affection for her was demonstrated. She implored him to marry again. Sobbing between each word, he replied: 'Non, j'aurai des maîtresses' – 'No, I shall have mistresses' – to which she responded: 'Ah! mon Dieu! cela n'empêche pas' – 'Oh God, that doesn't stop you'.

After her death, the king was inconsolable. He said he 'never yet saw a woman worthy to buckle her shoe'. George's daughters wondered how to comfort him. Walpole said he would send for Walmoden from Hanover, and that meanwhile the daughters should bring Lady Deloraine, a former mistress, to the king, for 'people must wear old gloves till they could get new ones'. The daughters were appalled by such crudity, but Walpole understood the soothing role, at this time of royal distress, which would be played by regular sex.

George gave Walmoden the title of Lady Yarmouth: the last royal mistress to be honoured with a life peerage. In an early, anonymous pamphlet of distinctly Jacobite sympathies, Samuel Johnson wrote of George's relationship with her: 'His tortur'd sons shall die before his Face, / While he lies melting in a lewd embrace.'

Once again after Caroline's death, people expected Walpole's downfall. Once again, he defied them. But his power was never quite the same. William Pitt and the 'Patriot Boys', as Walpole called them, clustered round the Prince of Wales, who like his father established a rival court at Leicester House. In 1739, Walpole was unable to avert the outbreak of what became known as the War of Jenkins' Ear against Spain – one of the insults by Spain having been the cutting off of the ear of Robert Jenkins, captain of an English merchant ship.

'They now ring their bells, but soon they will wring their hands,' Walpole predicted. And he was right: the war, fought at first in the Caribbean, began badly, which was blamed on him for not being enthusiastic enough. In 1742 he fell.

But George had at long last got his war, which soon broadened into the War of the Austrian Succession. In 1743, the sixty-year-old king led his army into battle against the French at Dettingen, on the River Main. His horse began by running away with him, almost into the enemy lines. George dismounted, placed himself at the head of his infantry, drew his sword and called in bad English on his men to charge. This was the last time a British king led his troops into battle. It greatly increased George's popularity.

In 1745, he again demonstrated his courage, by insisting that although the Young Pretender – also known as Bonnie Prince Charlie, the new Stuart claimant to the throne – had marched south from Scotland as far as Derby, there was nothing to worry about. George was right: the Jacobites were unable to raise the English against him, retreated to Scotland and the next year were cut to pieces at Culloden by an army commanded with merciless enthusiasm by the king's youngest and favourite son, the Duke of Cumberland, known to history as Butcher Cumberland.

George's heir, Frederick, the Prince of Wales, who had remained inveterately opposed to him and was one of the early patrons of the game of cricket, died in 1751. This event gave rise to the famous rhyme:

> Here lies Fred,
> Who was alive and is dead;
> Had it been his father,
> I had much rather;
> Had it been his brother,
> Still better than another;
> Had it been his sister,
> No one would have missed her;
> Had it been the whole generation,
> Still better for the nation;
> But since 'tis only Fred,
> Who was alive and is dead, –
> There's no more to be said.

Nor is there much more to be said about George II. He had all the wars he could want now. But to prosecute them successfully, he had to put up with William Pitt as his minister. And Pitt had the impudence to call for a 'blue water' strategy, a naval war in which Britain captured France's trade and became the world's leading maritime power. He defied George's demands for a continental land war in defence of Hanover, and denounced with implacable eloquence those ministers who were prepared to advocate such a strategy: 'It is now apparent that this great, this powerful, this formidable kingdom is considered only as a province of a despicable electorate.'

Pitt led Britain to great triumphs in the Seven Years War. Clive in India and Wolfe in Quebec won famous victories. But George was old now. On the eve of war, his ministers had pleaded with him to return from Hanover. He told them: 'There are kings enough in England. I am nothing there; I am old and want rest, and should only go to be plagued and teased there about that damned House of Commons.'

He died in 1760, and was the last king to be buried in Westminster Abbey. He left instructions that the side of his coffin, and the side of Queen Caroline's coffin next to it, should be removed. In death his ashes mingled with those of his altogether superior wife.

GEORGE III

1760–1820

This unhappy king is remembered for having lost America, and for having gone mad. He succeeded his grandfather at the age of twenty-two, and announced himself as a patriot: 'Born and educated in this country I glory in the name of Briton.' He was the first Hanoverian king to speak English with a native accent, and to show no desire to visit Hanover, where in a reign of just over fifty-nine years he never set foot. George instead showed a conscientious determination to do the right thing for Great Britain, and a frequent inability to see what that was.

As a boy, George was a slow developer, and did not learn to read until he was eleven. At the age of thirteen he became Prince of Wales, on the death of his father, poor Fred, eldest son of George II. The prince was dominated by his mother, Augusta, a pious German princess who suffered from exaggerated ideas of the respect due to royalty: when first presented to George II she hurled herself headlong on the floor. She inflicted on her eldest son a morbid sense of duty.

George conceived a violent admiration for his mother's friend, Lord Bute. When the young prince fell in love with Lady Sarah Lennox, the fifteen-year-old daughter of the Duke of Richmond, it was to Bute that he turned, with touching but misplaced sincerity, for advice: 'I submit my happiness to you, who are the best of friends, whose friendship I value if possible above my love for the most charming of her sex.' Bute advised against marrying this most charming girl, so George didn't.

When George ascended the throne, Britain was in the middle of winning vast new possessions in the Seven Years War. But the new king was under the unfortunate impression that the architect of victory, William Pitt, was a traitor. For Pitt had deserted the king's mother and gone instead to work for the king's grandfather. As usual, the Hanoverians were bitterly divided, generation against generation.

George III nevertheless respected some of George II's wishes: finding that his grandfather had left £6,000 in banknotes for Lady Yarmouth (George II's mistress, formerly known as Walmoden), the new king handed this money over, and added £2,000 of his own, whereupon Lady Yarmouth retired to Hanover.

Horace Walpole, son of the late Sir Robert Walpole, formed a good first impression of George III: 'His person is tall and full of dignity, his countenance florid and good-natured, his manner graceful and obliging.' George, who tended to prefer mediocre ministers, entrusted the running of the country to Bute. But Bute soon became very unpopular, and George realised he would have to be replaced: 'We must call in bad men to govern bad men.' Before long, Pitt was back.

His mother insisted he must marry a princess, so George put duty before pleasure and accepted Sophia Charlotte of Mecklenburg-Strelitz. She was short, thin and pale, with a prominent nose and a large mouth. But they stuck together and had fifteen children, of whom only two died young.

For the first time in English history, a monarch was admired for leading a frugal and virtuous family life, of the sort to which a God-fearing member of the middle class might aspire, and very different to the dissipations of an aristocracy addicted to gambling and government bribes. George believed in the virtues of fresh air, exercise and simple food. He and Charlotte liked to spend time at Kew, where they would rise at six in the morning in order to spend two hours alone together before breakfasting with their many children at the White House (now demolished) in what became Kew Gardens.

The king had a horror of obesity and between breakfast and dinner was accustomed to eat only a slice of bread and butter with black tea. He went for long walks and took a keen interest in agriculture, which led to his nickname of Farmer George. He also prayed by himself in a small chapel with his own prayer book, in which all references to 'our most religious and gracious king' had been struck out, and replaced with 'a most miserable sinner'. He was a profoundly devout Protestant, with a horror of Roman Catholicism. His religion led to a concern for education, so that every child could read the Bible, but also to the entrenched conviction that to allow Catholic emancipation would be a breach of his coronation oath.

The king's admirable private life was a hindrance when it came to understanding politics. Ministers found themselves assailed by John Wilkes, an outrageous libertine. They arrested Wilkes on a charge of seditious libel. Wilkes was unrepentant: he intensified his attacks, accused George of seeking to reintroduce Stuart despotism, and stood successfully for Parliament. The cry of 'Wilkes and Liberty' went up. George hated 'that devil Wilkes' and urged ministers to suppress him. Wilkes proved impossible to crush, for he expressed a new spirit of freedom.

The same inability to understand his opponents bedevilled the king's dealings with the American colonists. He saw that they defied lawful authority, and concluded that they were anarchists who must be brought to book. The minister who was supposed to achieve this difficult feat was Lord North, who like the king was a virtuous husband. For a dozen years, from 1770 to 1782, George sustained North in office.

As late as 1768, the Assembly of Virginia voted money for a statue of George III. But a decisive struggle was building over the right of the Westminster Parliament to levy taxes on the colonists. North tried to uphold the principle by imposing a duty on tea of threepence per pound, which was only a quarter of what English tea drinkers paid. In 1773 in Boston, people found this intolerable, and threw a cargo of tea in the harbour: the Boston Tea Party.

North closed Boston harbour and abolished the elected Council of Massachusetts: measures passed by large parliamentary majorities. Other colonies came in on the side of Massachusetts. In 1775, the Continental Congress met in Philadelphia, and the first skirmishes occurred in the neighbourhood of Boston, at Lexington, Concord and Bunker Hill. British casualities were uncomfortably high, but George called the colonists an 'unhappy, misled, deluded multitude', which was the general attitude in England. Wiser voices, such as Edmund Burke, who pleaded for a policy of conciliation with America, were drowned.

In 1776, in the Declaration of Independence, the colonists made their case: 'The history of the present King of Great Britain is a history of repeated injuries and usurpations, all having in direct object the establishment of an absolute Tyranny over these States. To prove this, let Facts be submitted to a candid world.' A list of more than two dozen offences, allegedly committed by George III, was followed by the words: 'A Prince whose character is thus marked by every act which may define a Tyrant, is unfit to be the ruler of a free people.'

A tyrant! This was an unbearable insult, and North set out to deal with the rebels. But there followed, in the years 1777–81, a series of British military disasters: Burgoyne blundered at Saratoga and Cornwallis at Yorktown. The French seized the chance to take revenge for the thrashing they had received at British hands in the Seven Years War, and lent decisive naval help to the rebels, as well as supplying almost all their ammunition. George's forces were humiliated, and North at last resigned.

How could any king recover from such a denunciation, followed by such a defeat? In 1780, his own Parliament had voted for Dunning's motion 'that the influence of the Crown has increased, is increasing, and ought to be diminished'. In 1782, George contemplated abdication, and again the following year, when he could see himself compelled to 'form a Ministry from among men who know I cannot trust them and therefore who will not accept office without making me a kind of slave'.

But time can bring great changes in the standing even of a king unjustly dismissed as a would-be tyrant. In order to avoid becoming the slave, as he saw it, of Charles James Fox, a great orator as dangerously liberal as Wilkes, George turned instead to William Pitt, son of the earlier Pitt.

In 1789 the French Revolution broke out. It seemed that like the Americans, the French might be about to gain their freedom, safeguarded by a constitution on the English model, but with checks and balances which would prevent the emergence of an overmighty king. Fox hailed the revolution as the greatest event in the history of the world. Burke denounced it, in his *Reflections*, as a lethal attack on every traditional source of authority.

And once the French king and queen had been executed, and the Terror had been unleashed, British opinion sided decisively with Burke. George himself saw the revolution as divine retribution for French support of the American colonists: a support which had indeed helped to bankrupt the French monarchy and make its collapse more likely.

Great Britain was now locked in a fight for survival against revolutionary France, led by an upstart general called Napoleon Bonaparte. George III became the figurehead of a civilisation that was in mortal danger. He himself suspected he would be the last King of England. His bouts of madness, of which the first had occurred as early as 1765, became more frequent and more prolonged, but so did his symbolic value. His eldest son hoped to take over from him, but was baulked by George's recovery: a story which will be told in the next chapter.

George's last public appearance was on 21 May 1811 at Windsor. Thereafter he was never seen outside the castle walls. The old man with a white beard had retreated into madness, as well as blindness and deafness. Wearing a purple dressing gown, he played to himself on the harpsichord. Then he stopped eating, and then he died. He had reigned longer than any English or British monarch before him.

GEORGE IV

1820–1830

No monarch since Richard III has received so bad a press as George IV. The Victorian age, which began a few years after his death, believed in thrift and marital fidelity. George by those standards was a monster: an out-of-control spendthrift who behaved with grotesque cruelty towards his wife. Yet his faults were normal enough among the eighteenth-century aristocracy, and he had a brilliant eye for the swagger, glamour and pleasure of gorgeous clothes and buildings. None of his successors has come close to matching his extravagant elegance, which helped him to invent the spectacle of the modern monarchy, and supply backdrops which are used to this day.

George was born on 12 August 1762 in St James's Palace. His father, George III, who was waiting nearby, was told by a confused official that he now had a baby daughter. He went to see, and found he had instead 'a strong, large, pretty boy'. Aged five days, the infant was made Prince of Wales, and at the age of three and a half, a Knight of the Garter. When he was four, his father presented him with twenty-one brass cannon, which fired one-pound balls. This was not, however, the preface to a brilliant military career. George showed little martial spirit, but evinced a gift for languages and mimicry.

He had a strict upbringing, but soon rebelled against his parents' tedious morality and frugality. At the age of seventeen he had an affair with Perdita, a famous actress some years older than himself to whom he had offered £20,000 to become his mistress. He never paid the money, she blackmailed him and the prime minister had to be persuaded to raid the secret-service fund to pay her off.

The king was annoyed by this, father and son became (as was usual for the Hanoverians) estranged, and the prince began to consort with opposition politicians such as Charles James Fox and the playwright Richard Brinsley Sheridan. The king blamed Fox for leading his son astray, and for developing in him a number of regrettable habits, which included vomiting in public, swearing in three languages, and displaying a total lack of financial self-control. Already the heir to the throne was showing his unsurpassed ability to spend money he did not have. He was determined to have the best of everything, and not think how it was to be paid for.

In August 1783, when he came of age, his debts were settled by Parliament, he was given his own establishment at Carlton House, near St James's Palace, which he set about rebuilding on a far grander scale, and he was granted an income of £60,000 a year. To set that sum in perspective, it is worth noting that HMS Victory, launched less than twenty years before and one of the most powerful warships in the world, cost £63,000, and prices had not risen all that much since that time. Yet the prince's debts were within three years over £250,000.

And he had fallen in love with Mrs Fitzherbert, a respectable Roman Catholic widow some years older than himself. She rejected his advances, and fled to the continent. 'Cursed with a truly royal lack of self-control,' as Max Beerbohm puts it, 'he was unable to bear the idea of being thwarted in any wish.' Every day he sent messages to Mrs Fitzherbert, imploring her to return and making formal offers of marriage. Yet to marry would require his father's consent, and he was in any case debarred by the Act of Settlement of 1701 from marrying a Roman Catholic.

Mrs Fitzherbert relented, and in 1785 they were married in secret. Very soon the secret was known, and the prince's debts became intolerable. George III refused to help. The prince responded by advertising to the world his destitution, and his affection. He closed Carlton House and drove to Brighton in a cab with Mrs Fitzherbert. William Pitt, as prime minister, tried to ease this scandalous situation by getting Parliament to pay the prince's debts, with the king making a contribution.

But in the autumn of 1788, the king's mind gave way. He talked without ceasing and could not sleep. When the prince was sent for, George III tried to throttle him. For two nights the prince sat up, beautifully dressed and waiting for his father to die. The father refused to die, but was confined to a straitjacket. The son looked forward to becoming Prince Regent, who would rule in his father's place.

Fox pressed for an immediate handover of power to the prince and himself. Pitt played for time. And then in February 1789, the king recovered, and became once more capable of transacting business. For his disloyal conduct towards his suffering father, the prince had become deeply unpopular. His coach was pelted by the London mob.

Part of the trouble was that the prince was given nothing to do. The long struggle against revolutionary France began in 1792, and would only end with the Battle of Waterloo in 1815. His younger brothers went into the army or navy, in which they attained high rank. The prince was only allowed to become colonel of the 10th Light Dragoons. He designed an exotic uniform for his regiment – designing uniforms was one of his passions – and for the manoeuvres near Brighton, he ordered a personal campaign tent in the form of a vast marquee emblazoned with the Prince of Wales's feathers, with some very expensive furniture to go inside it. His debts stood at £400,000, and by 1795 at £630,000.

There was only one way out of this desperate situation. He must bow to his father's wishes and marry a German princess. He agreed, sight unseen, to marry Princess Caroline of Brunswick. When he met her, he at once detested her, and retired to a distant part of the room. 'Harris,' he called to Lord Malmesbury, 'I am not well: pray get me a glass of brandy.'

The prince could not bear vulgarity, and perceived at once that his bride was unbearably vulgar: a cheap, brash, silly woman. She found him fatter than she had expected. The marriage ceremony took place in April 1795. The prince only felt able to go through with it by getting drunk first. On his wedding night, he fell asleep with his head in the grate. In the morning, he consummated the marriage. He said later that he slept only three times with Caroline, and she remarked on the large size of his cock, which led him to suppose she was not a virgin. Nine months later their daughter, Charlotte, was born.

For the rest of her life, Princess Caroline played the part of wronged wife with exhibitionistic brio. The public loved her, and hated her husband. Lady Jersey, a charming grandmother of forty-two, attempted to console the prince, but when she proved unable to meet in full his emotional requirements, he pleaded for, and obtained, the return of Mrs Fitzherbert.

In 1811, George III went irretrievably mad, and in 1812, his eldest son at long last became Prince Regent. He was generally regarded as a ludicrous, if not contemptible figure: a verdict that would continue to be passed on the monarchy for a quarter of a century.

But Great Britain was neither ludicrous nor contemptible. It led the coalition which in 1815, at Waterloo, inflicted final defeat on Napoleon. It had recovered from the loss of the American colonies, and possessed a worldwide empire. It led the Industrial Revolution, and was becoming the workshop of the world.

National self-esteem was bolstered by the possession of a constitution which seemed impervious to revolution, and by the abolition of the slave trade, which was proof of moral greatness. Cecil Woodham-Smith has described the sense of superiority which the country then possessed:

> British belief in the superiority of the British nation knew no bounds. It was an article of faith that one Englishman could beat six Frenchmen, more than six of any other foreign nation, and it was an almost religious conviction that the British possessed a sense of justice and fair play to be found nowhere else. An Englishman stood up for the weak, faced disaster without losing his head, kept his word and never kicked a man when he was down.

Perhaps this was why the nation felt it could tolerate a monarch who was so manifestly deficient. He came to suffer from the delusion that he had himself taken part in the charge of his regiment at Waterloo.

The Prince Regent was one of the great royal builders. His monuments include the Brighton Pavilion, the most fanciful edifice ever erected by a British monarch. He restored Windsor Castle, rebuilt Buckingham Palace, and set Nash to work in

London. In 1823 he presented to the nation a collection of 70,000 books assembled by George III, which became the nucleus of the British Library. In the same year, he persuaded the government to buy John Julius Angerstein's collection of pictures, which formed the basis of the National Gallery.

But he himself presented, after many years of gluttony, a figure so debauched that even the most elaborate corsets could no longer keep him in shape. He was known as Prinny, short for the Prince Regent, and Thomas Creevey, the diarist, wrote of him: 'Prinny has let loose his belly, which now reaches his knees; otherwise he is said to be well.'

In 1817, the Prince Regent suffered a terrible sadness. His only child, Charlotte, died after giving birth, at the end of a labour lasting fifty hours, to a stillborn son. The nation grieved for her: she was as popular as her father and grandfather were unpopular. But for her death, Charlotte would have become queen, and people believed she would purge away the many embarrassments inflicted on them by the House of Hanover.

The prince spent three months in deepest mourning at Brighton. He was now without an heir, and without any prospect of siring one. In January 1820, his father died, and he became king.

That summer, his dreadful wife returned from Italy, where she had been living with a handsome scoundrel called Bartolomeo Pergami, and attempted to claim her position as queen. She instead faced what became known as her 'trial' in the House of Lords – in fact an attempt by the king to divorce her. This prompted the usual demonstrations in her favour. In London, even the Duke of Wellington, the victor of Waterloo, found himself held up by recalcitrant workmen on his way back to Apsley House, and forced to drink Caroline's health. He did so with the words 'And may all your wives be like her.'

In July 1821, George IV was crowned in an immensely extravagant ceremony organised by himself with the help of the novelist Sir Walter Scott: the intention being to show that the British monarchy was more magnificent than Napoleon had ever been. Caroline attempted to gain entrance to Westminster Abbey, but was turned away on the typically English pretext that she had no ticket. Nineteen days afterwards she died.

George IV understood the importance of showing himself to his subjects. He had a successful visit to Dublin, for which he wore a field marshal's uniform of his own design, followed by a triumphal visit to Edinburgh, for which he appeared in full Highland dress. In George Street, at the top of the New Town, a handsome, greeny-black statue of him can still be seen, with his head turned towards what at the time of writing is a branch of Starbucks.

But his health could no longer sustain such public appearances. His ankles would not bear his enormous weight, and he was afflicted by gout and bladder problems. In 1826 he was visited at Windsor by his seven-year-old niece, Victoria, who was now, after his brother William, his heir. 'Give me your little paw,' he said to her, and invited her to ascend into his phaeton, in which he drove her at exhilarating speed.

In his last years, the public scarcely saw this wreck of a king. He at length gave way to Wellington on the vexed question of Catholic Emancipation, a measure needed to pacify Ireland.

George IV died on 26 June 1830. On his nightshirt, a miniature of Mrs Fitzherbert was found. The Times wrote of him: 'There never was an individual less regretted by his fellow creatures than this deceased king. What eye has wept for him? What heart has heaved one throb of unmercenary sorrow?' And this reflected the general view of one of the very few English monarchs who has ever had a profound feeling for the visual arts.

WILLIAM IV

1830–1837

William IV possessed no sense of royal dignity, and for the greater part of his life was not expected to become king. He was the third son of George III, and it was assumed that either his oldest brother, the Prince Regent, or his second brother, the Duke of York, would produce an heir. Only in 1817, when the Regent's daughter, Charlotte, died in childbirth, did it become likely that William would succeed.

For although the Duke of York had long been married to the Princess Royal of Prussia, they had no children and she instead lavished her affection on dogs, of which she had at least forty, as well as on monkeys, parrots, a llama and a kangaroo. The duke was commander-in-chief of the army, but had to be suspended for a time from that post when one of his mistresses was found to be selling commissions.

William was sent at the age of thirteen into the Royal Navy. He was already a convivial person, and said of his reception: 'I went to every part of the ship where I was received with universal joy.' He displayed bravery on active service and got to know the young Horatio Nelson, who would become as the victor of Trafalgar England's greatest naval hero. William said of him at this time: 'He appeared to be the merest boy of a captain I ever beheld.'

Nelson in turn said of William: 'He has his foibles, as well as private men, but they are far overbalanced by his virtues. In his professional line he is superior to near two-thirds, I am sure, of the list.' But William also tended to fall head over heels in love with a woman in every port, and acquired the crude naval vocabulary which was ever after to surprise some of those he met.

After about ten years in the navy, William came ashore, tried to become an MP, and was instead made Duke of Clarence by his father. William lived at first with the courtesan Polly Finch, but she could not stand his persistent readings from The Lives of the Admirals.

William instead set up house with Mrs Jordan, a famous actress with whom he lived for twenty years and had ten children, known as the Fitzclarences. Like his brothers, he got into debt. Mrs Jordan, who was said to have the best legs ever seen on the stage, bailed him out with her earnings. From time to time he would visit his brother, the Prince Regent, at the Brighton Pavilion, where the two of them would drink everyone under the table.

Although given the honorary rank of admiral, he was not thought to have good enough judgement to return to sea. His manners left much to be desired: the Duke of Wellington said William had 'personally insulted two-thirds of the gentlemen of England'.

His treatment at the end of Mrs Jordan seems to have been rather unfeeling: in 1812 he parted from her in order to contract a royal marriage, which he hoped would enable him to father an heir, and would certainly help to pay his debts. His choice fell, after various rejections, on Princess Adelaide of Saxe-Meiningen, of whom he wrote: 'She is doomed, poor, dear, innocent, young creature to be my wife.' Her frequent pregnancies unfortunately produced no surviving children, but she was good at managing her increasingly eccentric and impulsive husband, was a kind stepmother to the Fitzclarences, and established a fond relationship with William's niece, Princess Victoria.

In 1827, the Duke of York died. William became heir to the throne, and was seen at the funeral to be remarkably cheerful, for as he himself remarked: 'We shall be treated now very differently from what we have been.' The Duke of Wellington was appalled when a new prime minister, Canning, appointed William to the office of Lord High Admiral. William flung himself into naval reform, but after falling out with senior officers was forced to resign.

In June 1830, George IV died and William at the age of sixty-four became king. On his way to Windsor he laughed and greeted bystanders, his excitement overcoming his mourning for his brother, of whom he was genuinely fond. Princess Lieven remarked that the expression 'happy as a king' might have been invented for William IV, so much did he enjoy himself. He took an impromptu walk in the streets of London, was jostled by a mob and kissed by a whore, and loved it. When asked by his privy councillors to sign the declaration of his accession, he said in his informal, boisterous way: 'This is a damn bad pen you have given me.'

The new king looked quite odd. His head by common consent resembled a pineapple. The diarist Charles Greville described him as 'a kind-hearted, well-meaning, not stupid, burlesque, bustling old fellow, and if he doesn't go mad may make a very decent king, but he exhibits oddities'.

William did not go mad. He took a conscientious interest in his work, signing the backlog of 48,000 state papers left behind by George IV. The Duke of Wellington, who was prime minister, said he had done more business with William IV in ten minutes than with George IV in ten days.

A month after William ascended the throne, the French king was overthrown. Revolution was in the air. That year there were serious rural disturbances across the south of England, caused by low wages, bad harvests, an oppressive Poor Law and the introduction of the hated threshing machine, which was seen as a further attack on the livelihood of agricultural labourers.

The population had doubled since 1760, but the composition of Parliament was unchanged. Cornwall, with 300,000 inhabitants, elected forty-four MPs, while Birmingham, Manchester and Leeds, with half a million people between them, elected none. After the general election of 1830, William was reluctantly obliged to accept the resignation of Wellington and the appointment of Lord Grey as prime minister.

Grey brought in a bill for parliamentary reform. William was no reformer, but agreed to this. The Commons passed the Reform Bill by one vote, the Lords rejected it and the king sanctioned a quick dissolution of Parliament. The resulting general election produced a pro-reform Commons. William asked his ministers to modify the Reform Bill, and when they refused to do so, he continued to support them.

In September 1831 the king submitted to a coronation, though he called it 'a useless and ill-timed expense': his cost one-eighth of George IV's. In October, the Lords once more rejected the Reform Bill. Riots broke out, of which the most serious were in Bristol, where 400 people died. William with great reluctance agreed to create new peers, or at least to threaten to create new peers, unless the Lords passed the Reform Bill. In June 1832 it became law.

The king had done as his ministers wished. If he had not done so, it is unlikely that he would have remained king. He could still dismiss ministers: Melbourne suffered this fate in 1834. But this could only happen when the government lacked parliamentary support.

Not that William was incapable of asserting himself. When the president of the Royal Academy praised Captain Napier as 'one of our naval heroes', the king retorted: 'Captain Napier may be damned, sir, and you may be damned, sir, and if the queen were not here I would kick you downstairs, sir!'

William sacked his brother's French chefs and employed English ones. He loved entertaining: he would regularly have thirty people to dinner, and often a hundred. When he was in Brighton, he would look through hotel guest lists for naval comrades, and tell those he found: 'Come along directly. Do not bother about clothes.'

Lady Wharncliffe said: 'The king was in very good spirits and good fun, but one was afraid of encouraging him, as he was rather inclined to be improper in his jokes.' He loved to make lengthy after-dinner speeches, in the course of which he often became undiplomatic, as when he described the French king as 'an infamous scoundrel'.

When King Leopold of the Belgians was dining at Windsor, and preferred water to wine, William shouted: 'God damn it! Why don't you drink wine? I never allow anybody to drink water at my table!' But King Leopold was a Coburg, and William could not abide that jumped-up family of German princelings: least of all his sister-in-law the Duchess of Kent, the mother of Princess Victoria.

In the summer of 1837, William knew he was dying, and said: 'Doctor, I know I am going, but I should like to see another anniversary of the Battle of Waterloo. Try if you cannot to tinker me up to last out that day.' He died on 20 June 1837, two days after the anniversary of Waterloo.

VICTORIA

1837–1901

Queen Victoria reigned for longer than any of her predecessors. She rescued the monarchy from the contempt in which it was held in the early nineteenth century, and became the grand unifying figure, at once majestic and domestic, in a Britain which dominated the globe. Here was an empress who had a startling affinity with the middle class: the class to whose standards even the aristocracy now felt it must defer. Her views about politics, and especially about foreign affairs, were so strong, and expressed with such partisan sincerity, that it was impossible to kick her upstairs, to the less exciting region above politics which her successors came to occupy.

Her personality was of 'irresistible potency', as her greatest biographer, Lytton Strachey, put it. But to express, in a few pages, the contradictions of this shy, brave, passionate, truthful, dutiful, hysterical, self-controlled, self-indulgent, reckless, reticent, regal, modest, absurd, humorous, serious-minded, vulnerable, powerful and loveable woman is an almost impossible task. A guiding thread must be found, even at the risk of diminishing the richness of the bizarre mixture.

Victoria herself felt the need for a guiding thread, and found it in the morality of her times, conveyed by earnest-minded attendants such as her beloved governess, Baroness Lehzen, the daughter of a German pastor. No monarch has ever demonstrated a more sincere desire for self-improvement.

The pattern was set early on. When Victoria learned during a history lesson, at the age of eleven, that she would one day become queen, she declared after bursting into tears: 'I will be good.' Seven years later, in May 1837, she wrote in her journal: 'Today is my 18th birthday! How old! and yet how far am I from being what I should be.'

This desire to be what she should be was a marked change from her family's recent practice. Victoria's uncles were spendthrift libertines, who failed to produce legitimate heirs because they preferred to live with women whom they could not marry. Under the Royal Marriages Act of 1772, which remained in force until March 2015, any marriage by a member of the royal family required the consent of the sovereign.

Lord Melbourne, who was to serve as Victoria's first prime minister and as a father figure to her, explained to her the unfortunate effect of this law on her uncles: 'I don't wonder at their running wild, all very handsome young men; though that Marriage Act may have been a very good thing in many ways, still it sent them like so many wild beasts into society, making love wherever they went and then saying they were very sorry they couldn't marry.'

Victoria's own father, the Duke of Kent, was the fourth son

of George III. He went into the army, but imposed discipline with such 'bestial severity' that after the flogging to death of a sergeant, the rank and file conspired to murder him and he could be given no further employment. He shared with his brothers the defect of spending far beyond his income, and after living for a quarter of a century with a Frenchwoman, Madame de St Laurent, found himself so hopelessly in debt that he decided to take the desperate step of getting married. Parliament, he was confident, would then grant him a substantial income, in the expectation that in return he would provide an heir to the throne.

The duke's choice of bride fell on a German princess, Victoria of Saxe-Coburg, who had already been widowed once, and possessed two children. They were married in the summer of 1818. Ten months later, on 24 May 1819, their daughter, Victoria, was born. She never knew her father, for eight months later he died of pneumonia, contracted while spending Christmas at Sidmouth, on the coast of Devon.

Victoria's mother, the Duchess of Kent, fell under the thumb of the vulgar and greedy Sir John Conroy, the comptroller of her household. Conroy and the duchess were determined to control Victoria, but their clumsy attempts to do so cast a cloud over her childhood, and annoyed and alienated almost everyone. William IV was infuriated by them. At his birthday dinner in 1836, the king burst forth in a fury against the 'evil advisers' surrounding the duchess, and expressed the hope that power would pass directly to Victoria, on whom he doted.

He lived just long enough for his niece to attain, on her eighteenth birthday, her majority, and therefore to be able to reign in her own right, instead of submitting to her mother as regent. Early on the morning of 20 June 1837, Victoria learned from the Archbishop of Canterbury and the Lord Chancellor, who had hastened to her from the king's deathbed, that she was now queen.

The unknown sovereign made a brilliant first impression. At the swearing in, on her first morning, of her privy councillors, she impressed them by her air of self-possession shot through with modesty. Melbourne was on hand to explain, with his worldly wit, Victoria's new role to her, and to help dissolve every difficulty. The queen and her prime minister were soon very fond of each other. Even Dash, her spaniel, liked Lord M, and licked his hand.

To see the young queen, we must suppress for a moment the image of Victoria as a stiff, elderly widow dressed in black, who conceived it her duty never to smile when photographed. She was a pretty young thing, 'quite frisky' as she herself said, loved dancing and found she delighted also in her official duties. Thomas Creevey, who glimpsed her at Brighton, was charmed by her high spirits:

> A more homely little being you never beheld, *when she is at her ease*, and she is evidently dying to be always more so. She laughs in real earnest, opening her mouth as wide as it can go, showing not very pretty gums . . . She eats quite as heartily as she laughs, I think I may say she gobbles . . . She blushes and laughs every instant in so natural a way as to disarm anybody.

But at the beginning of 1839 this early success was blighted by scandal. Lady Flora Hastings, a maid of honour to Victoria's mother, made impertinent remarks about Baroness Lehzen, who had taken charge of the queen's household but possessed a number of easily mocked characteristics, including an uncontrollable urge to eat caraway seeds. When Lady Flora changed shape, it was in return put about that she was pregnant. Victoria herself believed this, as did Lord Melbourne.

But the rumour was not only malicious: it was false. Lady Flora turned out to be suffering from a fatal illness. The queen's enemies briefed against her in the press. Her popularity evaporated. She was hissed by aristocratic ladies at Ascot, and 'Mrs Melbourne' was shouted at her when she appeared on a balcony. The Duke of Wellington feared for the safety of the throne.

Melbourne was still at her side, but in May 1839 the dreadful prospect arose that she must lose him, and accept Sir Robert Peel as her new prime minister. Victoria was distraught. Peel struck her as chilly. He wished, for justifiable political reasons, to replace some of her ladies-in-waiting. Victoria was defiant: 'The Queen of England will not submit to such trickery.' Melbourne stayed in office for another two years.

In the autumn of 1839, Victoria's life changed forever. Her twenty-year-old cousin, Albert of Saxe-Coburg and Gotha, paid a visit to her at Windsor. She recorded in her journal her first impression of him: 'It was with some emotion that I beheld Albert – who is *beautiful*.' Five days later she proposed marriage to him. In February 1840, they were married, and her bliss was complete. 'My DEAREST DEAREST DEAR Albert,' she wrote in her journal, 'how can I ever be thankful enough to have such a *Husband!*'

The nation was less enchanted. Albert was seen as un-English: a charge impossible to rebut, for it was true. He was a German, from an obscure and distant duchy. He had no idea how to charm people, or even that it might be desirable to do so. He was capable of fox hunting, but had no time or inclination for the beloved sport of the English aristocracy. Instead he threw himself with Germanic earnestness into every kind of improving activity. The fact that he was very often right made him no more popular.

Albert and Victoria set out to create the happy home life which neither of them had enjoyed as a child. The queen had been fatherless, he was motherless. His father, the philandering Ernest I, Duke of Saxe-Coburg and Gotha, married a beautiful girl of sixteen whom he first neglected and then, when she sought consolation in other arms, banished forever: Albert last saw her when he was five.

The new husband, who was only twenty when he married, gradually made himself master in his own house, or houses, for in due course he and his wife took great pleasure in creating two entirely new residences: Balmoral in the Highlands of Scotland and Osborne on the Isle of Wight. After a dispute about the management of the royal nursery, Baroness Lehzen was prevailed upon to return to Germany.

Albert and Victoria had nine children. The queen loved sex, detested being pregnant, was not keen on babies but was fond of children. She took enormous care over their upbringing. The eldest, Vicky, responded well to Albert's plans for her. The next, known as Bertie, did not. The future Edward VII was a great worry to his parents, for he could not take life as seriously as they did themselves, and was unequal to the ambitious educational plans inflicted upon him by his father.

Soon Albert was fully involved in Victoria's political work. The highest title he enjoyed was Prince Consort, but in practice he became king. In a manner which is astonishing to modern eyes, Albert and Victoria did not hesitate to try to get rid of ministers of whom they disapproved. Lord Palmerston, as Foreign Secretary, was a particular bugbear: he had a disgraceful habit of encouraging the peoples of Europe to rebel against their kings, which in 1848, the year of revolutions, was a serious matter.

Albert was a moderniser, but he wanted to see liberal monarchies. He and Victoria were to become related in some way or other to every royal house in Europe: in the course of the nineteenth century the Coburgs colonised the continent. Albert married his eldest daughter, Vicky, to the heir to the Prussian throne, with the intention that Prussia too should become liberal. Vicky instead gave birth to a troublesome and ill-behaved child who as Kaiser Wilhelm II was to lead Germany into the First World War.

A much more successful project was the Great Exhibition of

1851, held in a vast glass building erected specially in Hyde Park. Albert oversaw every detail. Many people were infected by the same spirit of pessimism as was found in London before the 2012 Olympic Games: they feared the whole thing would be an embarrassing flop. The exhibition was instead a triumph, a demonstration to the world of Britain's commercial and industrial supremacy. Victoria was in ecstasies.

But Albert was not strong, and would not rest from his labours. He insisted on rising before dawn to work at his papers by the light of the green lamp which he had used as a student at the University of Bonn. He looked wretched, and had not yet managed to improve either the drains at Windsor, or the standard of the royal doctors, of whom the Foreign Secretary, Lord Clarendon, remarked: 'They are not fit to attend a sick cat.'

Prince Albert feared he would die of typhoid, an illness which at that time still carried off one in three people, and so he did in December 1861. Victoria was inconsolable. She went into mourning, and withdrew from the world. Each evening she had Albert's clothes laid out for him with hot water and a clean towel.

Her refusal to show herself to her people grew so protracted that a rising tide of republicanism began to make itself felt. She was known in disreputable newspapers as 'Mrs Brown', in reference to her fondness for John Brown, her retainer from Balmoral. What, the republicans asked, was the point, in an increasingly democratic age, of keeping at vast expense a monarch who was not even prepared to open Parliament? She in turn wondered why she should put herself out for a public who, despite the energetic production of every kind of Albert memorial, failed to appreciate her perfect husband at his full worth.

And then something very surprising happened. A politician was found who did appreciate Albert, and could tempt the queen from her seclusion. He was of Jewish descent, and as a young man had written glittering novels in which he showed a gift for applying medieval fantasy to the political and social conditions of the 1840s. Benjamin Disraeli knew how to salve her grief. 'The prince', he wrote to her, 'is the only person whom Mr Disraeli has ever known who realised the Ideal.'

In 1874, Disraeli began a six-year spell as her prime minister. He gratified her wish that she become Empress of India, and carried this into effect against much opposition. The monarchy was saved. She had re-emerged into public life as the representative, not of the most enduring empire the world had known – there Rome had set an unbeatable standard – but of the one with the largest number of square miles of territory.

Disraeli was elevated to the Upper House as Lord Beaconsfield, the name by which he referred to himself in this salutation on her sixtieth birthday:

> Today Lord Beaconsfield ought fitly, perhaps, to congratulate a powerful sovereign on her imperial sway, the vastness of her empire, and the success and strength of her fleets and armies. But he cannot, his mind is in another mood. He can only think of the strangeness of his destiny that it has come to pass that he should be the servant of one so great, and whose infinite kindness, the brightness of whose intelligence and the firmness of whose will, have enabled him to undertake labours to which he otherwise would be quite unequal.

One feels Disraeli enjoyed writing this as much as Victoria enjoyed reading it. To express his romantic veneration for royalty, tradition, splendour, in real life, and not just in the pages of a book, was a wonderful thing. As he lay dying in the spring of 1881, it was suggested to him that he might like to be visited by the queen. 'No,' he replied, 'it is better not. She'd only ask me to take a message to Albert.'

Disraeli was gone, but William Gladstone, his great opponent, lived on. Victoria could not bear Gladstone, telling her private secretary 'that she has the grtest [sic] possible disinclination to take this half crazy & really in many ways ridiculous old man' as prime minister. Take him she nevertheless had to do. But Gladstone had not the faintest idea how to manage Victoria: 'The queen alone is enough to kill any man,' as he complained to Lord Rosebery.

Relations between queen and prime minister reached a low point in 1884, when Gladstone refused to mount an expedition to rescue General Gordon, who had been sent to evacuate British forces from the Sudan, but was instead besieged by the Mahdi in Khartoum. Gladstone resisted the queen's urgings that a force be sent at once to save Gordon. When at last he yielded, it was just too late. Gordon was killed on 26 January 1885, two days before the relieving force arrived. Victoria was furious: as she wrote to her daughter, Vicky, 'it is I who have as Head of the Nation to bear the humiliation'.

The British Empire was subject to quite frequent humiliations of this kind. Empires always are. At the very end of her reign, the Boer War broke out, and British forces suffered a number of alarming defeats. But there was much to celebrate too, and at her golden jubilee in 1887, and her diamond jubilee in 1897, the queen became the focus of those celebrations. How the nation revelled in these declarations of its greatness, personified in the figure of the queen empress.

Her last prime minister, Lord Salisbury, with whom she got on very well, said of her after her death: 'I have always felt that when I knew what the queen thought, I knew pretty certainly what views her subjects would take, and especially the middle class of her subjects.' Democracy did not mean the end of monarchy, but required it to develop an alliance with the middle class.

EDWARD VII

1901–1910

E dward VII is the last monarch to have given his name to a period in British history. He epitomised an expansive and monied age of pleasure: of beautiful women, yachts, racehorses, country houses and portraits by John Singer Sargent. With imperturbable charm, Edward endorsed and rendered popular a diplomacy which aligned Britain with France rather than Germany. He led the reaction against all that was most earnest in Victorian England, and lent his name to a cigar, a potato and a district of Antarctica. But he took no interest in intellectual matters, and more delicate spirits, such as the caricaturist Max Beerbohm, saw in him a streak of intolerable vulgarity.

His parents had not intended that their eldest son, born on 9 November 1841, should turn out like this. Queen Victoria hoped 'to see him resemble his angelic dearest father in every respect'. Prince Albert devised a rigorous programme of education which would imprint on the young Prince of Wales's mind 'the principles of truth and morality'.

Bertie, as the boy was known in the family, was certainly not dim: he grew up fluent in German, English and French, and able to give a speech without notes in any of those languages. But while his elder sister, Vicky, lapped up the paternal curriculum, he detested it, and felt it as a kind of imprisonment. He was kept under strict supervision, and allowed to see no children apart from his siblings. Even during his studies at Oxford and Cambridge, he was not permitted to live in college. But on an early visit to Canada and the United States, he showed that he already possessed an astonishing capacity to charm almost all those with whom he came in contact.

At the age of nineteen, during a short period of training with the Grenadier Guards in Ireland, some of Bertie's brother officers smuggled an actress, Nellie Clifden, into his quarters. Albert heard of this escapade, and was deeply grieved by it. Although already ill, he went to Cambridge to remonstrate with his son. They were reconciled, but only a fortnight later, on 14 December 1861, Albert died. Queen Victoria placed some of the blame on Edward, and wrote of him to his older sister, Vicky: 'oh, that Boy – much as I pity, I never can or shall look at him without a shudder'.

Edward managed, by his tact and evident grief at his father's death, to some extent to overcome this maternal revulsion. But for the next forty years the queen never allowed him to play the slightest role in politics.

He instead became the leader of society. He married the beautiful Princess Alexandra of Denmark, and in due course indulged his appetite for women with an ample supply of mistresses, generally recruited from the upper classes. His circle was rich, raffish, sometimes scandalous: its adulteries amused and horrified the public, especially when Edward himself was obliged to appear in the witness box. But when he recovered from a serious illness in 1871, people were so relieved that the incipient republican movement faded away.

For Edward had a kind of magnanimity. He got on well with Sir Charles Dilke, a prominent English republican, and did not mind that the French had got rid of their monarchy: he loved being in Paris. In 1901, when he ascended the throne, Britain's reputation in Europe was at a low ebb because of the Boer War, which looked like the mighty British Empire trying with clumsy brutality to tyrannise the plucky Dutch settlers in southern Africa.

As king, Edward first worked for an Anglo-German alliance. His efforts failed, in part because of the attitude of his nephew, Kaiser Wilhelm II, who deeply resented Britain's greatness. British policy turned then to an alliance with France: the Entente Cordiale of 1904. Edward prepared the way with a visit the previous year to that country, where he was at first met with cries of 'Vive les Boers'. But so well did he communicate his love of France that within a few days this changed to 'Vive notre roi'.

Edward announced at the outset that he intended to reign as a constitutional monarch, and he stuck to this. He never tried to sack a minister. But he did lend strong support to reform of the army and the navy. Admiral Jackie Fisher, who was introducing the new dreadnought battleships in the face of stiff resistance, said Edward VII's public support 'just simply shut up the mouths of the revilers'.

The king took a close interest in clothes, and rebuked anyone he found incorrectly dressed. This extended to the prime minister, Lord Salisbury, who had a mind above clothes and appeared one day at Buckingham Palace in a strange mixture of uniforms. Edward flew into a rage and shouted: 'Here is . . . Europe in a turmoil – twenty ambassadors and ministers looking on – what will they think – what *can* they think of a premier who can't put on his clothes?' To which Lord Salisbury replied that it was a dark morning and 'I am afraid that at the moment my mind must have been occupied by some subject of less importance'.

Because he became very fat, Edward stopped doing up the bottom button of his waistcoat: a custom other men imitated, and which has lasted to this day. He ate enormous meals of many courses, smoked huge numbers of cigars and cigarettes, but drank only in moderation. He loved women, shooting, racing and yachting. On one of his frequent visits to the spa town of Marienbad, Edward's private secretary, Frederick Ponsonby, was confronted by 'a beautiful lady from the half-world of Vienna who wanted the honour of sleeping with the king. On being told this was out of the question, she said that if it came to the worst, she could sleep with me.'

When things went wrong, Edward was a calming influence. After the Dogger Bank Incident of 1904, when the Russian fleet shelled some English trawlers under the mistaken impression that they were Japanese warships, Edward asked: 'Are we prepared to go to war for the sake of the heirs of two harmless fishermen?'

His reign ended with a political crisis of the first magnitude. The House of Lords defied the House of Commons and voted down the People's Budget, which introduced much heavier taxes on the rich to fund an extension of welfare for the poor. The monarch was drawn into this row, because he had to decide whether or not to threaten to create so many hereditary peers that the Lords could be defeated.

The king was appalled by this idea, which to him meant taking sides and abandoning royal impartiality. He became depressed, spoke of abdicating, and took the view that his son would be the last king. But in the middle of the great struggle between the Lords and the Commons, Edward VII died from a series of heart attacks. On one side of his deathbed was Queen Alexandra; on the other, his mistress, Mrs Keppel.

The king lay in state in Westminster Hall: an innovation which, his official biographer, Sir Sidney Lee, noted, 'proved extremely popular'. A quarter of a million people filed past the coffin. For while the political power of the monarchy had declined, its ceremonial impact at weddings, coronations, funerals and other big occasions was increasing: a process David Cannadine identified in his brilliant essay on the British monarchy and the invention of tradition.

Edward VII was the central figure in this development: he was determined that British ceremonial should no longer be outshone by the kaiser's Germany, and one of his earliest acts was to revive as a grand public occasion the state opening of Parliament. Lord Esher organised the great state pageants of the Edwardian period, and the Church of England learned how to conduct gracefully immaculate services in place of the slipshod and unrehearsed occasions seen in the past. Sir Edward Elgar composed sublime music to accompany every state occasion.

Lord Northcliffe, a pioneer of popular journalism, noted that by 1908, the press was devoting five times as much space to royalty as at the start of Edward VII's reign. Far from being left behind by the new, mass-circulation newspapers such as the Daily Mail, this monarch provided them with some of their best copy.

GEORGE V

1910–1936

George V was an exceptionally dutiful, unpretentious, unimaginative naval officer, who helped to see his country through great perils. He was born in 1865 and was fond of both his parents. The Prince of Wales – the future Edward VII – was an indulgent father, who allowed his children to race pieces of hot buttered toast down his trouser crease. Princess Alexandra was a doting mother, who continued to address her son as if he were a small child long after he was grown up.

Until the age of twenty-six, George did not expect to become king, and instead pursued a naval career. At the age of twelve, he joined the training ship *Britannia* along with his older brother, Eddy. Life as a cadet was hard: as he later recalled, 'It never did me any good to be a prince.' He rose to command first a torpedo boat and then a gunboat.

But at this point, Eddy died and George came ashore. For the rest of his life he kept the beard, the trousers pressed from side to side, and the bluff manner which he had acquired in the navy. His sense of rectitude prompted a hatred not just of unpunctuality, but of any form of spontaneity: characteristics which were to make him harsh towards his own children.

He married Princess May of Teck, a great-granddaughter of George III. She had first been engaged to the apparently empty-headed Eddy. As queen, she altered her first name from May to Mary. In her view, 'No member of our family should smile in public': a dictum which imparted a certain joylessness to royal photographs long after the death of Queen Victoria, who had likewise disapproved of smiling for the camera.

Harold Nicolson, who wrote the official life of George V, lamented of his subject: 'For seventeen years before his accession, he did nothing at all but kill animals and stick in stamps.' George amassed one of the great stamp collections. When a courtier asked him, as Prince of Wales, if he had seen that 'some damned fool has paid £1,400 for a stamp', he replied: 'Yes. It was this damned fool.' The stamp was the Mauritius 2d blue.

George V ascended the throne at a time of political peril which was to last for the next four years, until the outbreak of the First World War gave people worse things to think about. In 1910 he had to decide whether, in order to stop the Lords blocking the wishes of the Commons, he would threaten to create more peers: the same question which William IV had faced at the time of the Reform Bill. George V agreed with reluctance to do so.

In Delhi, the new king and queen held a magnificent durbar, at which the Indian princes paid homage to him as emperor: the first and last time such a ceremony was to be held. George wrote in his diary: 'Rather tired after wearing the crown for 3½ hours, it hurt my head as it is pretty heavy.'

Once the royal couple had returned to Britain, the miners, dockers and railwaymen went on strike. The suffragettes were also up in arms, and at the 1913 Derby, Emily Davison killed herself by throwing herself under the king's horse. The queen's first thought was for the jockey: 'Poor Jones.' Ireland was sliding into civil war, with Ulster Unionists determined to resist by force the imposition of an Irish Parliament.

In 1914, Max Beerbohm described in a letter to his wife the demeanour of the king and queen at the state opening of Parliament:

> And after they had passed I found myself with tears in my eyes and an indescribable sadness – sadness for the king – the little king with the great diamonded crown that covered his eyebrows, and with the eyes that showed so tragically much of effort, of the will to please – the will to impress – the will to be all that he isn't and that his Papa *was* (or seems to him to have been) – the will to comport himself in the way which his wife (a head taller than he) would approve. Oh such a piteous, good, feeble, heroic little figure. I shall never forget the sight.

In August 1914, the First World War broke out. The king wrote in his diary: 'It is a terrible catastrophe, but it is not our fault . . . Please God it may soon be over & that he will protect Bertie's life.' Bertie, his second son, the future George VI, was serving in the Royal Navy. His oldest son, the future Edward VIII, was in the army, but was not permitted, to his great annoyance, to serve in the front line, and was instead attached to the staff.

During the war, George V personally conferred 50,000 decorations, held 450 inspections, visited 300 hospitals and went five times to visit the armies in France. His horse was startled, on one of these visits, by a sudden cheer from some servicemen, reared up, threw him and then fell on him, fracturing his pelvis: an agonising injury. Like his father, the king took a detailed interest in uniforms, and had strong views on what would and wouldn't do. When some uniforms for the RAF band were shown to him, he commented: 'Porters at a cinema!'

After Lloyd George complained of drunkenness among munitions workers, the king became teetotal: 'I hate doing it, but hope it will do some good.' This measure was announced in April 1915 as 'the King's Pledge', and made life at court even more arduous, especially as food was in such short supply that one could not afford to arrive even a moment late for breakfast or one would get nothing.

The king did not wish to see a vengeful attitude towards the Germans. The First World War was among other things a family quarrel: the kaiser was his first cousin. But so strong was anti-German feeling in Britain that it was deemed wise to change the family name from Saxe-Coburg-Gotha to Windsor. The kaiser thought this was absurd, and said he was looking forward to seeing 'The Merry Wives of Saxe-Coburg-Gotha', but in Britain the change was popular.

Tsar Nicholas was likewise a first cousin of George V: their mothers were sisters, and the two monarchs were very fond of each other. Yet when the Bolshevik revolution occurred, the king questioned the government's proposal that the tsar and his family should take refuge in England. It is in any case doubtful whether the tsar would have agreed to such a plan.

Nicholas and his family were murdered by the Bolsheviks at Ekaterinburg in July 1918. George V was grief-stricken. These were precarious times to be a king. Within a few months, the defeat of Germany and of the Austro-Hungarian Empire had led to the overthrow of the Hohenzollerns and of the Hapsburgs. Yet in London in November 1918, the king and queen drove for five successive days in an open carriage through cheering crowds to celebrate victory.

In the early 1920s, the Labour Party was in the process of replacing the Liberals. But socialism did not turn out to be as alarming as the Russian example suggested. British Labour politicians were as anxious to demonstrate respectability as the king was to confer it. In January 1924 the first, short-lived, Labour government was formed. The king wondered what his grandmother, Queen Victoria, would have thought, but was himself favourably impressed: 'I must say they all seem to be very intelligent & they take things very seriously. They have different ideas to ours as they are all socialists, but they ought to be given a chance and ought to be treated fairly.' Here was the king as the upholder of the national idea of fair play. Like a cricket umpire, he could be depended upon to do his best to remain impartial.

In October 1924, the Conservatives returned to power. But the miners were determined to go on strike in protest at cuts in their wages. In July 1925, George wrote in his diary: 'I fear a strike at the end of the week. It will play the devil in the country. I seem never to get any peace in this world. Feel very low and depressed.' The king expressed to ministers his sympathy with the miners, and advised against harsh measures.

The following year, the General Strike took place, when workers in many other trades for nine days supported the miners.

The king wrote: 'Our old country can well be proud of itself as during the last nine days there has been a strike in which 4 million men have been affected; not a shot has been fired and no one killed: it shows what a wonderful people we are.'

In 1928 the king nearly died of a pleural abscess, and the following year he had a relapse brought on by laughing at the jokes of J. H. Thomas, a former railwayman who had become his favourite Labour politician. The Great Depression opened with the Wall Street Crash of 1929, and overwhelmed the efforts of the Labour government of 1929–31 to deal with it by orthodox economic measures including spending cuts.

In 1931, the prime minister, Ramsay MacDonald, tendered his resignation, but was instead persuaded by the king to lead a National Government. While most of the Labour Party regarded this as an act of treachery by their leader, the king advised MacDonald to 'brace himself up to realise that he was the only person to tackle the present chaotic state of affairs'.

The king's staunchest defenders did not pretend he was an amusing man. They praised his common sense, and pointed out that his tact and modesty saved him from getting things wrong. He was proud of using the same collar stud for fifty years, and when it broke, he got it repaired.

At Sandringham, he chose to live for many years in a poky house called York Cottage: the sort of place which might appeal to a philistine stockbroker. It is said that serving in the navy had given him a taste for confined spaces. The king noticed that his own sons spent as little time as they could at Balmoral. He asked J. H. Thomas why this was so, and received the reply: 'It's a dull 'ouse, sir, a bloody dull 'ouse.'

Max Beerbohm composed, for private circulation, a poem in which a lady-in-waiting and a lord-in-waiting argue with each other, she insisting, 'The queen is duller than the king,' to which he retorts, 'The king is duller than the queen.' H. G. Wells sneered at 'an alien and uninspiring court', to which the king retorted: 'I may be uninspiring but I'm damned if I'm an alien.' His son and heir, the future Edward VIII, said his father believed 'in God, in the invincibility of the Royal Navy, and the essential rightness of whatever was British'. The king could not, unfortunately, say anything as reassuring about Edward, but instead remarked to the Archbishop of Canterbury: 'After I am gone the boy will ruin himself in twelve months.'

In 1932, George V began the Christmas broadcasts which moved at once from being a popular innovation to a popular tradition, and have continued to this day. These enhanced his status as the father figure who united the far-flung parts of the British Empire. On 6 May 1935 the king and queen drove to St Paul's for a silver-jubilee service of thanksgiving. In the East End of London, the king was received with such affection that he remarked: 'I'd no idea they felt like that about me. I am beginning to think they must like me for myself.'

On 20 January 1936 the king died at Sandringham, his passing accelerated by his physician, Lord Dawson of Penn, who had strong views about when would be the most dignified hour for his master to expire. The king's funeral procession included Charlotte, his parrot since his days in the navy, who was transported in a cage in one of the carriages.

EDWARD VIII

1936

In January 1936, when he ascended the throne, it appeared to many people that Edward VIII was in an ideal position to modernise the monarchy. He was wildly popular as Prince of Wales, and far more up to date than his father, George V. Born in 1894, he suffered as a child from a sadistic nurse, and was educated at home by an uninspiring tutor before being sent to Osborne Naval College, and afterwards to Magdalen College, Oxford, which he left without taking a degree.

At the outbreak of war, in 1914, he was twenty years old, so was just the right age to go and fight, as he wished, with the army in France. But this to his great disappointment he was not allowed to do. When he pointed out that he had three younger brothers, so it would not matter if he were killed, the reply came that the real problem would come if he were to be taken prisoner. So he was made to serve with the staff, making only occasional visits to the front line. His embarrassment was increased by the award of a Military Cross which he felt he had not earned.

In the years of peace after 1918 he was sent on tours of the world, and especially the large parts of it which belonged to the British Empire. He charmed the crowds, and showed what looked like genuine concern for the unemployed.

But in newsreels and photographs, the glamorous prince wears a look of pained and barely veiled boredom. He detested ceremonial occasions, and the bright, rich, fashionable and somehow aimless people among whom he tried to enjoy himself were not much better. It was an empty life. He took mistresses, but this did not make him more contented. His preference was for older women who were already married. For a long time he showed no inclination to get married himself. It is possible that a bout of mumps when he was an adolescent had left him infertile.

His courtiers were dismayed by their vain, restless, petulant employer. In 1927, his assistant private secretary, Tommy Lascelles, warned the prime minister, Stanley Baldwin, that 'the heir apparent, in his unbridled pursuit of wine and women, and what-ever selfish whim occupied him at the moment, was rapidly going to the devil, and unless he mended his ways, would soon become no fit wearer of the British crown'.

After the prime minister agreed to this, Lascelles went on to say that when the prince was riding in a point-to-point, he 'couldn't help thinking that the best thing that could happen to him, and to the country, would be for him to break his neck'. Baldwin replied: 'God forgive me, I have often thought the same.' Lascelles resigned in 1929, unable any longer to tolerate the prince's behaviour, but returned in 1935 to work for George V.

Edward and his younger brother, who became George VI, were almost unbelievably ignorant not just of intellectual and artistic life, but of English literature. During a tour of Dorset, the prince visited Thomas Hardy at Max Gate, the novelist's home near Dorchester:

> Conversation flagged, and to reanimate it the Prince of Wales said brightly, "Now you can settle this, Mr Hardy. I was having an argument with my Mama the other day. She said you had once written a book called *Tess of the d'Urbervilles*, and I said I was sure it was by somebody else." Thomas Hardy, like the perfect gentleman he was, replied without batting an eyelid, "Yes, sir, that was the name of one of my earlier novels."

In 1934, the Prince of Wales took a new mistress: Wallis Simpson, a thin, ambitious, thirty-eight-year-old American, who had already been divorced once, and was now married to Ernest Simpson, a businessman. Edward was besotted by her. He derived an intense but even to his friends incomprehensible satisfaction from flinging himself at the feet of a woman who was not very attractive. Perhaps her unsuitability was what attracted him. She would test whether his people really loved him. And if they didn't, he could shed the intolerable burden of kingship.

Even before he ascended the throne, the prince displayed a sympathy with the fascist regimes in Germany and Italy which went beyond British government policy. But it was his determination to marry Mrs Simpson that towards the end of 1936 brought matters to a head. On 27 October she and Mr Simpson were divorced, which left her free to marry the king. Some people objected to Edward VIII marrying a woman who had two former husbands still living, while others were more appalled that she was an American.

Edward seems to have imagined that as king, he could continue to separate his private life from his public duties, just as he had done while Prince of Wales. Baldwin, as prime minister, told him that this was not possible, and insisted that 'in the choice of a queen the voice of the people must be heard'.

On 3 December 1936, when the British press broke its silence about his love affair, the king was shocked to discover widespread hostility to Mrs Simpson. This hostility was fully shared by the royal family: they detested her. When his mother, Queen Mary, asked him to reflect on the damage his behaviour would do to his family, to the throne and to the British Empire, Edward replied: 'Can't you understand that nothing matters – nothing – except her happiness and mine?' The king had some supporters, notably Winston Churchill, but nothing like enough to make a fight of it, even if he had wished to do so.

On 10 December he signed the Instrument of Abdication, and on the evening of the following day he made a broadcast which had in part been written by Churchill. It included the line: 'I have found it impossible to carry the heavy burden of responsibility and to discharge my duties as king as I would wish to do without the help and support of the woman I love.' According to Tommy Lascelles, Edward 'really loathed being king, and was determined to get out of it as soon as he could'.

Baldwin at the head of the Establishment had reached the conclusion that Edward would not do, and that the next brother down, the altogether quieter and more conscientious Duke of

York, would make an acceptable replacement. The Dominions – notably Canada, Australia and South Africa – took the same line.

Here, one may note, was a chance to get rid of the monarchy altogether. James Maxton, an Independent Labour MP, duly proposed in Parliament that Britain should become a republic. His motion was defeated by 403 votes to 5. Neither the ruling class nor the people wanted Britain to take that route. Baldwin himself described the monarchy as 'the guarantee against many evils'. What people wanted was a conscientious monarch.

Edward VIII took the title of Duke of Windsor. He married Mrs Simpson, so she became the Duchess of Windsor, after which he so pestered George VI with demands that she be given the title of Her Royal Highness that in time the new king refused to take his predecessor's calls. Relations never recovered. When George VI died, the Duke of Windsor came to the funeral, but appeared 'jaunty', and in a letter to his wife referred to his own mother, and his sister-in-law, as 'these ice-veined bitches'. The newly widowed queen was known to believe that if Edward VIII had not abdicated, her husband would still be alive. The duke died in 1972, and the duchess in 1986. The most charitable view to take is that the immensely onerous role to which he had been born was too much for him. His precipitate departure meant that 1936 was the first year since 1483 with three monarchs.

GEORGE VI

1936–1952

George VI had no desire to be king. For the first forty years of his life he was overshadowed by his older brother, and his good qualities were undervalued even by himself. As a child, he developed a stammer. His father, George V, whose fondness for his children was generally concealed by a rigid and irascible attachment to routine, was annoyed by his son's inability to speak, and would tell him, 'Get it out.' But a stammer does not obey orders, and Bertie, as he was known to his family, remained troubled by this agonising affliction for many years to come: a particular burden for someone required to give speeches, and even to make live broadcasts.

In January 1909, at the age of thirteen, he joined the Royal Navy as a cadet. His health was bad: he had gastric troubles which eventually ended his naval career. But he was able, at the age of twenty, to serve in the forward gun turret aboard HMS *Collingwood* at the Battle of Jutland. This was the decisive naval engagement of the First World War, for despite suffering heavier losses the Royal Navy retained its mastery of the seas and drove the German fleet back into port.

Soon after the war, George asked Lady Elizabeth Bowes-Lyon, daughter of the Earl and Countess of Strathmore, to marry him. She hesitated: she belonged to an ancient family of Scottish aristocrats, and was herself a strong-minded woman of unusual vivacity and charm. There was no need for her to expose herself to the intrusions which marrying a member of the royal family would entail.

But when George made his third attempt, she accepted him. In 1926, their first child, Elizabeth, was born, and in 1930 their second, Margaret Rose. The four of them lived a happy family life. George's older brother, who would become Edward VIII, often came to see them. Then Mrs Simpson came on the scene. No one except Edward could stand her, but in December 1936 he abdicated in order to marry her.

George's mother, Queen Mary, later recounted how 'appalled' her second son was to become king: 'He was devoted to his brother and the whole Abdication crisis made him miserable. He sobbed on my shoulder for a whole hour – there, upon that sofa.'

On the morning of 12 December 1936, King George VI read out the following declaration at his Accession Council:

> I meet you today in circumstances which are without parallel in the history of our Country. Now that the duties of Sovereignty have fallen upon me I declare to you My adherence to the strict principles of constitutional government and

My resolve to work before all else for the welfare of the British Commonwealth of Nations. With my wife and helpmeet by My side, I take up the heavy task which lies before Me.

The new queen had a gift for enjoying herself, and for being seen to enjoy herself. The new king, brought up to admire his brother's crowd appeal, was nervous that he would be found inferior. But his speech therapist, Lionel Logue, who had worked with him since 1926, helped him to surmount the horrors of speaking in public. And most importantly, the public very much wanted the king to succeed: they saw a dutiful man who was doing his best, and they supported him. If that had not been the case, no amount of striving by George VI to do the right thing would have been of much use.

The new king and queen were strong supporters of the policy of appeasement. At the end of September 1938, when the prime minister, Neville Chamberlain, returned from Munich, proclaiming 'peace with honour' after agreeing that Hitler should seize the part of Czechoslovakia which rendered that country defensible, he was invited by George VI to appear with him on the balcony of Buckingham Palace. The crowds cheered with wild enthusiasm.

But it soon emerged that Hitler had not, after all, been appeased. In August 1939, when he invaded Poland, Britain went to war. In May 1940, Chamberlain's position became untenable, and he was replaced by Churchill. The king and queen would have been happier if Lord Halifax, the altogether more emollient Foreign Secretary, had taken over.

Churchill had been one of Edward VIII's most outspoken supporters. But he was 'a most vehement royalist' and was soon on good terms with George VI. The Blitz began, and on 13 September Buckingham Palace was bombed, with the king himself witnessing the attack: 'We all wondered why we weren't dead. Two great craters had appeared in the courtyard.' This produced a valuable sense of national togetherness.

The king and queen toured the areas of London and other cities that had suffered the worst bombing. 'Never in British history', Time magazine reported, 'has a monarch seen and talked to so many of his subjects or so fully shared their life.' The war, it was said, was the making of George VI. But if one man symbolised Britain's determination to fight on in 1940 after France had fallen, and before either Russia or America had entered the war, it was Churchill.

As soon as the war in Europe was won, the British people dismissed Churchill. They wanted the peace to be built by the Labour Party. George VI accommodated himself to this change. He did his duty as a constitutional monarch, while also fearing that the old world of country houses was passing away. The empire too was starting to pass: in 1947, India became independent and the king stopped being emperor. But in the same year, the marriage of the king's daughter helped to reconcile the Labour Party to the royal family.

The king was very tired after the war, and not at all well. He was a heavy smoker, a custom that would help to kill him at the age of fifty-six. He loved shooting, at which he was exceptionally good. He remained very interested in decorations and uniforms, and took not the slightest interest in books or the arts. But he got on well with some at least of the Labour people. He found it very funny when Ernie Bevin, the Foreign Secretary, said on being asked if he would be taking his wife to a conference in Paris: 'Taking Mrs Bevin to Paris is like taking a sandwich to a banquet.' On 6 February 1952, the king died in his sleep after an enjoyable day's shooting at Sandringham. He had become, especially in the war years, a fitting representative of a nation which feared it was getting, in relative terms, weaker. By sheer pluck he kept going.

ELIZABETH II

1952–2022

Elizabeth II continued the conscientious monarchy which her father, George VI, had restored after the Abdication crisis. In her youth, she received immoderate praise without becoming unhinged, and was acclaimed by President Truman when she visited the White House as 'a fairy princess'. But in later decades, her quiet virtues – fidelity, modesty, keeping going without fuss – ceased to be fashionable, and she had a daughter-in-law, Diana, Princess of Wales, who was fashionable.

The queen had attained a position above fashion as well as above politics. People found it almost impossible to disrespect her. Even the most hardened satirist, more than ready to go for her children, tended to retire discomfited from the attempt to take a crack at Elizabeth II. For to disrespect her was to declare oneself brazen, unkind, disreputable, a bit of a lout.

She was born on 21 April 1926 at 17 Bruton Street, London home of her mother's parents, the Earl and Countess of Strathmore. The chances of her becoming queen seemed at this point remote: it was expected that her father's older brother, the future Edward VIII, would get married and have children, and even if he didn't, her own parents, the Duke and Duchess of York, might have a son who would take precedence over her. But they, as it turned out, had a second daughter, Margaret Rose, born four years later.

Elizabeth's early life was that of an upper-class girl who learned good manners, Christian piety, how to dance and speak French, the enjoyment of games such as hide and seek, and the love of animals. Intellectual life was considered superfluous, if not harmful. The essential thing was to be initiated into a tradition of behaviour.

The two children had no friends of their own age, but Lilibet, as she was known in the family, was passionately fond of horses and dogs. In 1936, a book called *Our Princesses and their Dogs* was published, with the approval of her parents, containing photographs of the four of them with their eight dogs: two corgis, three yellow Labradors, a Tibetan lion dog, a golden retriever and a black cocker spaniel. The text, by Michael Chance, conjures a lost world of deferential sentimentality:

All these dogs live together on terms of perfect amity, if one excepts the occasional tendency of Dookie [one of the corgis] to disturb the harmony of the scene by his somewhat arrogant but none the less lovably amusing attempts to impose his will on Choo-Choo [the Tibetan lion dog] or, for that matter, on any of the other dogs who may be so foolhardy as to arouse his ire. Dookie, in other words, is the 'character' of the party, and as such is the avowed favourite of Princess Elizabeth and her mother.

Nevertheless, as is stated elsewhere, the two princesses, their parents and their dogs constitute one very human and happy family . . . Moreover, just as we humans know that in all the world there are no royalties so unselfconscious as our own, none so considerate of others, so devoid of artificiality, so rich in human qualities, it may well be that Dookie and Jane [the other corgi], being dogs of sense, instinctively share our knowledge.

Thanks to Marion Crawford, who for sixteen years was the girls' governess, we possess an eyewitness account of the queen's childhood. In 1950, Crawfie, as she was known, published *The Little Princesses*, an affectionate memoir which was regarded by George VI's wife as an act of gross and unpardonable betrayal. We glimpse the ruthlessness with which she protected her family. Crawfie, who did not die until 1988, never saw or heard from any of them again.

Royal biographers have often belittled her and her book. But Crawfie saw more of Princess Elizabeth than any of them ever have, and describes, with enchanting perceptiveness, the making of a dutiful monarch. On arrival, Crawfie found Alah Knight, the duchess's family nanny, in charge of the nursery: 'She was what every good nurse ought to be – calm and kind, exuding that comfortable air of infallibility and security so necessary to the welfare of the young.'

Crawfie gives a truthful account of the 'very sour-natured' Dookie: 'He bit me once quite severely, and on another occasion took a piece out of Lord Lothian's hand. With great fortitude his lordship averred it was nothing! It did not hurt him at all. "All the same, he bled all over the floor," Lilibet pointed out.'

The Duke and Duchess of York did not live in an ostentatious way: 'In general, a complete absence of any kind of lavishness was the family rule.' Lilibet's dutifulness can be seen from the care with which she looked after her collection of about thirty toy horses: 'Stable routine was strictly observed. Each horse had its saddle removed nightly and was duly fed and watered. No matter what else might be going on, this was a must-be-done chore.' Crawfie sometimes grew alarmed by her charge's conscientiousness: 'She became almost too methodical and tidy. She would hop out of bed several times a night to get her shoes quite straight, her clothes arranged just so. We soon laughed her out of this.'

When her grandfather, George V, dies, Lilibet looks up from one of her toy horses and says, 'Oh, Crawfie . . . ought we to play?' Clouds gather over the family, for the duke's older brother, who is now king, has fallen in love with Mrs Simpson: 'As usual, nothing whatever was said . . . Maybe the general hope was still that if nothing was said, the whole business would blow over.'

To Crawfie falls the task of diverting the young princesses from what soon developed into the greatest crisis to afflict the monarchy in the twentieth century: 'I do not know what we would have done at that time without the swimming lessons.' At the end of 1936, Lilibet's uncle abdicated and her father with great reluctance became king. They had to move from their family home at 145 Piccadilly to Buckingham Palace, which 'rather resembles camping in a museum'.

In May the next year, when her father is crowned in a long service at Westminster Abbey, Lilibet worries that Margaret will fall asleep in the middle: 'After all, she is *very* young for a coronation, isn't she?' But Lilibet is able to report afterwards: 'She was wonderful, Crawfie. I only had to nudge her once or twice when she played with the prayer books too loudly.'

One finds almost intolerable strain being borne by concentration on detail: a method any of us might use, but perhaps of particular value in the training of a constitutional monarch, whose public duties are often appallingly dull, and require an unwearying capacity to focus on minute particulars if they are to be performed with grace rather than embarrassment. In 1939, at the age of thirteen, she started to take lessons in British constitutional history from Sir Henry Marten, the vice-provost of Eton.

That summer the royal family went on a cruise along the south coast of England in the royal yacht, *Victoria and Albert*. They anchored off Dartmouth Royal Naval College and here Elizabeth met, for the first time, Prince Philip of Greece. He had recently enrolled as a naval cadet, and was an impoverished member of the Greek royal family, which was of Danish descent, though like most European royalty he was also descended from Queen Victoria. Philip was eighteen, and Elizabeth was impressed, according to Crawfie, by how high he could jump. He seems to have enjoyed impressing her: when the royal yacht sailed away, he rowed after it long after all the other small boats had obeyed the signal to turn back. They began to write to each other.

The princesses spent the Second World War at Windsor Castle, which was safer than staying in London. Their father was protective of them, but they enjoyed taking part in amateur theatricals. At the end of the war, Elizabeth was allowed to don uniform and train in vehicle maintenance with the Auxiliary Territorial Service.

Prince Philip saw service in the Royal Navy in the Mediterranean and Pacific. He was mentioned in dispatches, saw Elizabeth while on leave, and they became closer. Her father said it was too soon to think of marriage, but at Balmoral, in the summer of 1946, Philip proposed to her and she accepted him. They were not permitted to announce the engagement, for early the next year, the king and queen were to visit South Africa with their two daughters, and Elizabeth's twenty-first birthday was to be marked by an act of dedication from which no distraction would be tolerated.

On 21 April 1947 Princess Elizabeth broadcast by radio the following words, which Tommy Lascelles, the king's private secretary, had arranged to be drafted for her by Dermot Morrah, a distinguished member of *The Times*'s editorial staff. Here was the spirit in which she intended to reign:

> There is a motto which has been borne by many of my ancestors – a noble motto – 'I serve'. Those words were an inspiration to many bygone heirs to the throne when they made their knightly dedication as they came to manhood. I cannot do quite as they did. But through the inventions of science I can do what was not possible for any of them. I can make my solemn act of dedication with a whole empire listening. I should like to make that dedication now. It is very simple. I declare before you all that my whole life whether it be long or short shall be devoted to your service and the service of our great imperial family to which we all belong.
>
> But I shall not have the strength to carry out this resolution alone unless you join in it with me, as I now invite you to do: I know that your support will be unfailingly given. God help me to make good my vow, and God bless all of you who are willing to share in it.

The key phrase here was 'my whole life whether it be long or short': Princess Elizabeth assured her future subjects that her course was set. She returned home and got married to Prince Philip. They soon had their first two children: Charles born in 1948 and Anne in 1950. Two other children, Andrew and Edward, followed somewhat later. For a short time, she was able to live a relatively normal life as the wife of an able and energetic naval officer. But in February 1952, while she and her husband were in Kenya, at the start of a tour which was supposed to take them to Australia and New Zealand, they received the news that George VI had died.

The queen, as she now was, returned to London. Her husband became the Duke of Edinburgh and had to give up his naval career: for him a severe sacrifice, which he must have hoped would come later, for his father-in-law was only fifty-six years old. The rest of their lives would be dominated by the duties of a sovereign and her consort.

The coronation, held in 1953, was the first great spectacle of the television age. The presence of the cameras enforced high standards: because the event was going to be seen by many millions of people, it was rehearsed in minute detail. Gone was the slovenly confusion of Queen Victoria's coronation in 1838. A democracy expected better than that, and revelled in the sonorous commentary provided by Richard Dimbleby. Ancient (or partially ancient) ceremonies and the latest technology complemented one another.

The royal family was left on a dangerously exposed pinnacle of adulation. This could not last, for the family was composed of human beings who were bound to get into difficulties, often of a marital nature. Princess Margaret, younger sister of the queen, fell in love with a divorced man, Group Captain Peter Townsend, who had worked for George VI, and of whom her whole family were very fond.

Should she be allowed to marry him? The Church of England's opposition to the remarriage of divorced people remained as strong as it had been in 1936, when her uncle wished to marry Mrs Simpson. The Times published a leading article which ended with the sententious observation 'that happiness in the full sense is a spiritual state and its most precious element may be the sense of duty done'.

Duty clashed with inclination, and in 1955, after much agonising, duty won. The queen's sister did not marry Townsend. She afterwards got married to Anthony Armstrong-Jones, a photographer, from whom she later got divorced.

In 1957, Malcolm Muggeridge wrote an article in which he suggested that the queen and her family had become 'a kind of royal soap opera' or even 'a sort of substitute or ersatz religion'. Today such sentiments seem unremarkable, but at that time they prompted an explosion of anger against Muggeridge for casting doubt on the royal fairy tale.

Most of the later reporting of the royal soap opera does not deserve to take up space here. Excessive deference yielded to outrageous impertinence. The media became more and more shameless. When the Duke of Edinburgh dismissed them to their faces as 'scum', the royal correspondent of the Sun newspaper responded: 'Yes, but we are the crème de la scum.' Scraps of inaccurately regurgitated royal gossip sold many millions of newspapers and magazines. The declining power of the officer class, to which the queen's husband and father both belonged, left her much more exposed than at the start of her reign, when wartime habits of patriotic self-restraint were still prevalent. To the satirists of the 1960s, the officer class looked ridiculous, given to saying things like: 'We need a futile gesture at this stage. It will raise the whole tone of the war.'

A very big royal story was the marriage in 1981 of Charles, Prince of Wales, to Lady Diana Spencer. They did not know each other well, and after a beautiful wedding, and the birth of two sons, found themselves unable to bear the sight of each other. In private life, this situation quite often arises, but their life did not remain private.

They were drawn into a public wrangle which became unbearably painful and unbearably vulgar. The queen encouraged them to get divorced, for that step had become unavoidable. They did so, but not long afterwards, the princess was killed in a car accident in Paris. This was the cue for a public outpouring not only of grief, but of anger with the queen, who was unable to express such grief. Her ingrained reticence affronted many, though by no means all, of her subjects. Her prime minister, Tony Blair, had to step in with a public tribute to 'the people's princess', and with shrewd advice to the queen about how to make concessions to popular feeling.

Two other of her children also got divorced. One could argue that these troubles put the royal family in touch with modern life, where marriage had become a less hallowed institution. But the catalogue of failure must also have been horrible for the queen. In November 1992, just after part of Windsor Castle had burned down, she gave a speech to mark the fortieth anniversary of her accession in which she said: '1992 is not a year on which I shall look back with undiluted pleasure. In the words of one of my more sympathetic correspondents, it has turned out to be an *annus horribilis.*'

After these convulsions, a gradual but unmistakable recovery occurred. In 2011, the queen made the first state visit by a British monarch to the Republic of Ireland, which was a great success, for she struck exactly the right reconciling note. In 2012, she entertained a vast public by seeming, in a film shown at the opening of the London Olympics, to arrive at the stadium by parachuting from a helicopter along with James Bond, played by Daniel Craig.

Part of the charm of monarchy is that it is at one and the same time precarious and stable. No one really knows what will happen next, but everyone can express an opinion. The queen continued to take delight in her dogs and her horses, and seldom looked happier than when going racing.

Her devotion to the Commonwealth, which for much of her reign seemed like a nostalgic remnant of imperial feeling, began to look like an astute way to maximise the United Kingdom's global connections. She was a global as well as local figure. At the start of her reign, the Commonwealth had eight members; at the end it had fifty-six, with a total of 2.2 billion inhabitants, and she was still queen of fifteen of them: the United Kingdom, Canada, Australia, New Zealand, Jamaica, the Bahamas, Grenada, Papua New Guinea, Solomon Islands, Tuvalu, St Lucia, St Vincent and the Grenadines, Belize, Antigua and Barbuda, and St Kitts and Nevis.

Her life was a paradox. She had authority, yet was powerless. People find this difficult to understand. The same phenomenon is found in religion, which to the queen meant much more than it did to a large proportion of her subjects. The supreme governor of the Church of England continued to tell us about her Christian faith, as in this passage from her Christmas Broadcast in 2014: 'For me, the life of Jesus Christ, the Prince of Peace, whose birth we celebrate today, is an inspiration and an anchor in my life. A role model of reconciliation and forgiveness, he stretched out his hands in love, acceptance and healing. Christ's example has taught me to seek to respect and value all people of whatever faith or none.'

She was brought up as a Christian, and as a Christian monarch she reigned. In 2020, she broadcast words of comfort to the nation during the ordeal of the Covid pandemic: 'We will be with our friends again. We will be with our families again. We will meet again.' The following year, the Duke of Edinburgh, her husband of seventy-three years, died at the age of ninety-nine, and she was seen sitting alone, in accordance with Covid regulations, at his funeral. Her own health slowly faded. People knew the end must come, but dreaded it. On 6 September 2022, at Balmoral, she invited Liz Truss, the last of her fifteen prime ministers, to form a government, and two days later she died.

Charles III

2022–

Charles III waited longer than any of his predecessors to become king. While setting this record, he found it intolerable merely to go through the motions of being a dutiful heir, and felt moved to take a passionate interest in farming, the environment, architecture, the inner cities, medicine, music and things of the spirit. Here was an establishment figure who often found himself compelled to voice, with anguished sincerity, his opposition to the establishment view.

The popular press ridiculed his preoccupations and took a relentless interest in his love affairs, his marriage in 1981 to Lady Diana Spencer, and the collapse of that marriage. She had a charisma unmatched by the Windsors, but died in 1997 in a late-night car crash in Paris while pursued by photographers. In 2005 the prince at long last married the woman he had loved and lost before he met Diana, Camilla Shand, and she, as far as anyone could see, made him happier than he had ever been, and helped him with grace and confidence to ascend the throne.

Charles was born in Buckingham Palace on 14 November 1948. When he was three his grandfather, George VI, died, and when he was four he attended his mother's coronation in Westminster Abbey, where he was looked after by his beloved grandmother, the Queen Mother. His most vivid memory of that great ceremony was the palace barber cutting his hair too short and making it lie flat by applying 'the most appalling gunge'.

Soon after his fifth birthday, his parents departed on a six-month tour of the Commonwealth which took them to Bermuda, Jamaica, Fiji, Tonga, New Zealand, Australia, Ceylon (now Sri Lanka), Aden and Uganda. He followed their progress on a globe, and with his younger sister, Anne, rejoined them when they reached Malta, where in the Grand Harbour Britain's mighty Royal Navy, commanded by his uncle, Lord Mountbatten, steamed in review past the royal yacht *Britannia*.

The little prince was observed by those close to him to be 'terribly sensitive': he responded well to kindness, but retreated within himself when treated roughly. In what was considered a daring act of modernisation, he became the first heir to the throne to be sent away to school rather than kept at home in the hands of a tutor or governess. His education was placed in the hands of his father, the Duke of Edinburgh, who had thrived at Gordonstoun, on the Moray Firth, as one of the first pupils there of Kurt Hahn, a brilliant German Jewish educationalist. But Hahn had gone by 1962, when Charles arrived, and the prince was bullied unmercifully, with anyone who tried to make friends with him accused of sucking up and he himself describing life as 'absolute hell'. Things improved some years later when a new master, Eric Anderson, recognised the prince's considerable gifts as an actor, and cast him in the title role in *Macbeth*.

In 1966, he spent two enjoyable terms at Timbertop, in Australia, and the following year he went up to Trinity College, Cambridge, to read archaeology and anthropology. Here too he broke new ground: no previous heir to the throne had been allowed to live in college. But modernisation, difficult enough at any time, was especially tricky in the 1960s, when to be young and fashionable meant throwing off the whole fusty inheritance of rules, inhibitions and class-based convention.

Many a shy English youth struggled in these years with the question of how far to break with the code of his parents' generation, but none had to navigate these conflicting currents in such a glare of publicity as the prince. While at Cambridge he acted in some mildly satirical sketches, but felt no inclination to follow most of the fashions of the time. He got to know Harry Williams, Dean of Chapel at Trinity, who preached astonishing sermons published as *The True Wilderness*, and later said of Charles:

> I always thought he was a deep person, that he wasn't taken in by the surfaces of life. He had an interest in the deeper things of life, in the source of life, an openness of mind, a readiness to evaluate ideas, not taking things off the peg but thinking them out for himself . . . It may sound absurd but I always thought he had the makings of a saint when he was young: he had the grace, the humility and the desire to help other people.

The title Prince of Wales had been conferred on Charles when he was only nine years old, and eleven years later he went through a faintly embarrassing investiture ceremony at Caernarvon Castle, devised by his uncle, Lord Snowdon, who was married to the queen's sister, Princess Margaret. The prince was plainly doing his best, and had learned enough Welsh while studying for a term at Aberystwyth to be able to deliver a speech in that language, but the Welsh Nationalists professed to be outraged.

He now served briefly in the RAF, quickly becoming a pilot, and for some years in the Royal Navy, where he was at length put in command of a minesweeper, HMS Bronington. But after that, what was he to do for the rest of his life? He had glamorous girlfriends, and pursued with enthusiasm various sports, such as hunting, shooting, polo and skiing, which led the press to acclaim him as the world's most eligible bachelor and a man of action. In a moment of weakness, he had suggested that thirty was a good age to get married, which for him meant 1978. He was under pressure, and knew that whoever he married would have to accept a lifetime of public duties and press intrusion.

In the autumn of 1980, the press learned that the prince had become friends with Lady Diana Spencer. She was only nineteen years old, and was at once besieged by photographers. Charles was faced, as his father pointed out, with a choice: either he get engaged to her, or he end the relationship. In February 1981, the prince took the risk and proposed. She took the risk and accepted. Few people realised at this point that they were entirely incompatible, but in order to protect her from the press she was moved into a suite of rooms in Buckingham Palace, where she at once felt lonely and miserable, and neglected by her fiancé, whose diary was full of longstanding official engagements, including a five-week visit to Australia and New Zealand.

The press wrote this up as a fairy-tale romance, and most

people believed it was, though when an interviewer on the day the engagement was announced said he supposed they were in love, Diana replied, 'Of course,' while Charles added, in a fond tone, 'Whatever "in love" means.' In July 1981, they had the 'wedding of the century' in St Paul's Cathedral, a vastly popular event. The princess gave birth to William in June 1982 and Harry in September 1984. She had star quality, and an astonishing gift of empathy with people she scarcely knew, or did not know at all, but she and Charles did not get on. 'They don't pull together,' one observer said sadly. It was much worse than that: they were both desperately unhappy, and were pulling apart. Via an obliging journalist, Diana told the world of her sorrows with the prince, who had remained attached to an old love of his, Camilla Parker Bowles (née Shand). Via another obliging journalist, the prince told his side of the story.

He no doubt felt wounded by the false account of his behaviour which had been supplied to the press. Nor could he say to his calumniators, as the great Duke of Wellington once said, 'Publish and be damned.' He needed, as the heir to the throne, to be visible, and not hopelessly unpopular, and could only remain so with the help of the media. One might ask, as did the author of *The Leopard*, Giuseppe di Lampedusa, whether in these times it was any longer possible to be a prince, when no one knew what a prince was. A large part of the public sided with the princess throughout this period, saw her as the injured party when the royal couple got divorced in 1996, and were thrown into transports of grief when she was killed in Paris in 1997, while fleeing with her then boyfriend from a posse of press photographers.

The prince flew to Paris to bring her body home, and walked with their sons, aged only fifteen and twelve, behind her coffin to her funeral in Westminster Abbey, at which Elton John sang and her brother, Lord Spencer, gave an address in which he said her 'blood family' would look after William and Harry. Seldom had London witnessed such an outpouring of infuriated sorrow.

But determined though the princess's supporters were, they could not maintain their fury at boiling point indefinitely, and in 2005 the prince felt able to marry Camilla in a civil ceremony at Windsor Town Hall. Her great-grandmother, Alice Keppel, had been the last mistress of his great-great-grandfather, Edward VII, twenty-nine to his fifty-six when they met and at his bedside when he died aged sixty-eight, and she understood how to calm his angry moods. Camilla, twenty-five to Charles's twenty-four when first they fell in love, could calm his moods. He did not at that early point have either the sense or the daring to ask her to marry him, and was posted by the Royal Navy to serve for eight months in the West Indies, during which time she got engaged to Andrew Parker Bowles, a dashing and well-connected officer in the Household Cavalry.

These romantic convulsions distracted the press, and have distracted the present author, from Charles's quest for wisdom. All his life he has sought for spiritual truth, and has turned to those who might provide it. He loves Shakespeare and the Book of Common Prayer, and has a deep knowledge of sacred music, of which he is an influential patron. From his earliest years, he felt a deep love of nature, and a fear that mankind, with arrogant disregard for the environment, was wrecking the planet. In town after town he saw architects, developers and councillors suppose it was best to tear down traditional buildings and erect soulless monstrosities in their place. In the face of such destruction he could not remain silent. With astonishing courage and insensitivity, he in 1984 protested, in a speech at the 150th anniversary dinner of the Royal Institute of British Architects, at a proposed extension to the National Gallery, describing it as 'a monstrous carbuncle on the face of a much-loved and elegant friend'. The prince set up schools where traditional architecture and drawing could be studied, built Poundbury in Dorset to show what could be done, and stopped the carbuncle, but for many years his efforts did not seem to bear much fruit.

Princess Diana was uninterested in such matters, and resented the time he devoted to them. He himself recognised that his interventions often seemed to achieve nothing. 'Perhaps,' he said in a speech in 1982 to the British Medical Association, 'we just have to accept that it is God's will that the unorthodox individual is doomed to years of frustration, ridicule and failure in order to act out his role in the scheme of things, until his day arrives and mankind is ready to receive his message.'

In 1993, he said in a letter to the director of the Prince's Trust, one of his charities: 'I have always wanted to roll back some of the more ludicrous frontiers of the 1960s in terms of education, architecture, art, music and literature, not to mention agriculture.' He wrote endless letters in which he lobbied ministers on these subjects. When these letters were at length published, they were found to contain many sensible and tactful suggestions. He cared deeply about the welfare of his country and his world.

Charles, his admirers said, was schooling himself to become a philosopher king. His critics feared he would exceed his powers. Nobody could be certain he was exceeding his powers as Prince of Wales, for that role was, as he himself lamented, entirely undefined. Like a superfluous man in a nineteenth-century Russian novel, he felt appalled by many aspects of the society into which he had been born, but powerless to do anything about it.

Bagehot, writing when Victoria was on the throne, said the monarch had 'the right to be consulted, the right to encourage, the right to warn'. That was a good description of what Charles did as Prince of Wales. He often warned, was anxious to encourage, and insisted on being consulted. No royal figure since Prince Albert has striven with such sincerity to raise the standard of

British culture in so many different fields. His reward was to be accused of being a meddlesome prince who would become a meddlesome monarch. In 2015, his private secretary, Sir William Nye, found it necessary to write to The Times to declare: 'After half a century in public life, few could be better placed than His Royal Highness to understand the necessary and proper limitations on the role of a constitutional monarch.'

The queen at length died and Charles succeeded her. His benevolent manner calmed the fears of many who had wondered whether he could fill the gap she left. It became apparent that most people wanted him to make a success of his new role, and that as king he possessed an authority which had eluded him during his long years as heir. His manner with crowds was warm, and unlike his deeply lamented mother, he was happy to be touched by members of the public, and would himself stretch out a hand. On a visit to Westminster Hall he picked up the stick which an old lady had dropped. He and Camilla made a successful state visit to Germany, a country of monarchical temper which he and his mother had often visited.

His coronation, held in May 2023, was an even greater success. His insistence that Camilla be crowned queen beside him was accepted almost without demur. The Anglican Church conducted the service, and knew how to make other faiths welcome, as did the king. The hereditary peerage had lost the leading role it used to play at coronations in support of the hereditary monarchy, but the costumes and coaches were still gorgeous, the marching still splendid and immaculate. The music, much of it commissioned by the king, was sublime. Rachel Cooke wrote in the following day's Observer:

I confess to tearfulness when Charles, now in a plain linen shirt, knelt before the altar; and later on, as he put his arms into his gold robe, there was something so tender in the manner of the churchmen who dressed him. The king's studied helplessness was peculiarly moving; in that moment, he had an invalid quality, a feeling that he was moving beyond something – though what that something might be, precisely, I cannot say.

She spoke for many who did not think of themselves as monarchists, and were astonished to find themselves so moved. The mystery of kingship had been shown to a people few of whom had ever seen a coronation. After many wanderings and agonies, Charles III had come into his own.

AFTERWORD

Why Has the British Monarchy Survived?

Few writers about the royal family are able to shed much light on this question. Some of them imagine, on observing the dutifulness with which Elizabeth II conducted herself, that the monarchy has survived because of the virtues of individual monarchs. Their attitude is that of courtiers: they wish to see the best in their sovereign, and in the case of this queen, they do not find themselves short of material.

Other writers go to the opposite extreme. They are determined to mock the monarchy. Their great aim is to demonstrate that they have not themselves been taken in by an indefensible anomaly. In a democratic age, they consider the monarchy to be an absurd anachronism. They are surprised it has not been abolished, and assume it soon will be. Such attitudes are often held by intellectuals, and by writers of comedy programmes for BBC Radio 4.

Both approaches are wrong, or at best inadequate. Neither the loyal courtier nor the contemptuous intellectual sees to the heart of the matter.

The main reason the monarchy survives is that we the people want it to survive. We have a popular monarchy, created, maintained and modified by popular demand. In that sense, it is our most democratic institution.

As Eric Hobsbawm, a communist rather than a monarchist, observed in his essay on the mass production of traditions in Europe from 1870 to 1914: 'Glory and greatness, wealth and power, could be symbolically shared by the poor through royalty and its rituals.' By magnifying the monarch, we magnify ourselves.

Which is why republics, even great and successful ones such as the United States, so often find themselves apeing monarchical forms. The president of the United States is an elective monarch, who at times also acquires hereditary characteristics. The Americans got rid of George III, but could not expunge their desire and even their need for a king.

I do not say the British monarchy could survive anything, but these pages show it has survived an awful lot. If we did not wish it to exist, we would within about five minutes come to see it as entirely intolerable. Perhaps one day we will.

Meanwhile it commands general acceptance because it gives us things democratic politics cannot supply. We feel reassured by a source of authority that does not change every few years at an election. Our politicians are by their nature transitory. We invite them to solicit our votes by promising to solve our problems, and within a few years we condemn them for letting us down, and kick them out.

We have kicked unsatisfactory monarchs out too, most recently in 1936. But as Parliament grew in power, the sovereign withdrew and began to be seen as 'above politics'. By a mixture of accident and design, our monarchs conducted, one might say, a brilliant political manoeuvre. The king or queen continues to represent us, without having to stand for election.

This does not square with democratic theory, according to which legitimacy springs from getting the most votes. But it does square with human nature, which requires a person on whom to focus our deepest loyalties. And in some ways it is easier, one might even say fairer, if that person has been chosen by accident of birth, than by some supposedly meritocratic process which is monopolised by a gang of scrabbling careerists.

Religion often requires obedience to a person: in Christianity, to Christ the King, or Lord, of creation. And in the United Kingdom it still seems natural and fitting for judges, members of the armed forces, Members of Parliament and candidates for British citizenship to swear obedience to the monarch.

We prefer to swear allegiance to a person who is not a politician. Many of us hate politicians. We consider them to be a lot of crooks who are 'all the same'. By soliciting our votes, they have demeaned themselves.

The monarchy has become one of the greatest, though least observed, checks on arbitrary power. It occupies the space which a dictator would need to occupy. Because it is unthinkable in Britain to push the monarch aside, tyranny itself becomes unthinkable. In countries where for understandable reasons the monarchy was overthrown – France in 1789, Russia in 1917, Germany in 1918 – tyranny was not unthinkable.

How much easier the hereditary principle is to accept. It relieves the monarch of the accusation of having set out to attain the highest position in the state. And however objectionable it may be in strict democratic theory, it is in practice widely observed, for most of us hope to pass on whatever possessions and abilities we may have to our children and our children's children.

We are interested in the monarch's family in a way we are seldom interested in the family of a politician. For this family unites us with someone far above us in the hierarchy. We too are born and marry and die. Here is a way in which without boasting we can consider ourselves the equals of the royal family, condemned to a common human fate. As Bagehot observed in *The English Constitution*, 'A family on the throne is an interesting idea . . . A princely marriage is the brilliant edition of a universal fact, and, as such, it rivets mankind.'

Even convinced republicans can occasionally be found reading news about members of the royal family doing nothing very much. But writers about politics tend to be obsessed by power. Because the monarch appears to have little power, they are uninterested in him. They do not see that as the guarantor of the constitution, and the undisputed focus of national loyalty, he is in many ways the lynchpin of the whole system. Far from being a vestigial anachronism, he is an essential part of the structure. He is not just decorative, but useful.

This book contains examples of monarchs who overestimated their strength, conceived that it was their duty to do things their people regarded as intolerable, and were therefore overthrown. Politics is a constant repetition, in cycles of varying length, of making kings, and then killing them in order to achieve a kind of rebirth. The survival of the House of Windsor depends on its continuing willingness to surrender this sacrificial role to the politicians.

ACKNOWLEDGEMENTS

My greatest debt is to David Birt, who taught me history at Abberley Hall School, and placed a lifetime's knowledge at my disposal. This book is dedicated to him. I am indebted too to Basil Morgan, the always encouraging and amusing head of history at Uppingham School; and to my supervisors when I read history at Trinity College, Cambridge, including Walter Ullmann, Brian Wormald, Jonathan Riley-Smith, Shirley Letwin and Norman Stone. Thomas Kielinger, author of a fine biography of Queen Elizabeth II in German, allowed me the run of his royal library. James Knox lent *Our Sovereigns* by Osbert Lancaster, published in 1936, and Craig Brown *Philip and Elizabeth* by Gyles Brandreth, published in 2004. It would be invidious to select from the vast number of other works which I have consulted a few for praise, and absurd to attach to so personal a book a scholarly apparatus. Professor Jeremy Black, of Exeter University, offered valuable advice. I am indebted to Ginda Utley and Susan Clarke for help with particular points, and to the latter for much information about Charles III. My agent, Andrew Gordon, urged me to write popular history and proposed monarchs as a subject. Rosemary Davidson, at Square Peg, took on the book, and saw how it should be done. She suggested we ask Martin Rowson to make his brilliant drawings. My brother, David Gimson, who teaches history at Cheney School in Oxford, read the manuscript and detected a number of errors. My wife, Sally Gimson, sustained me through innumerable difficulties. All blunders are my own.